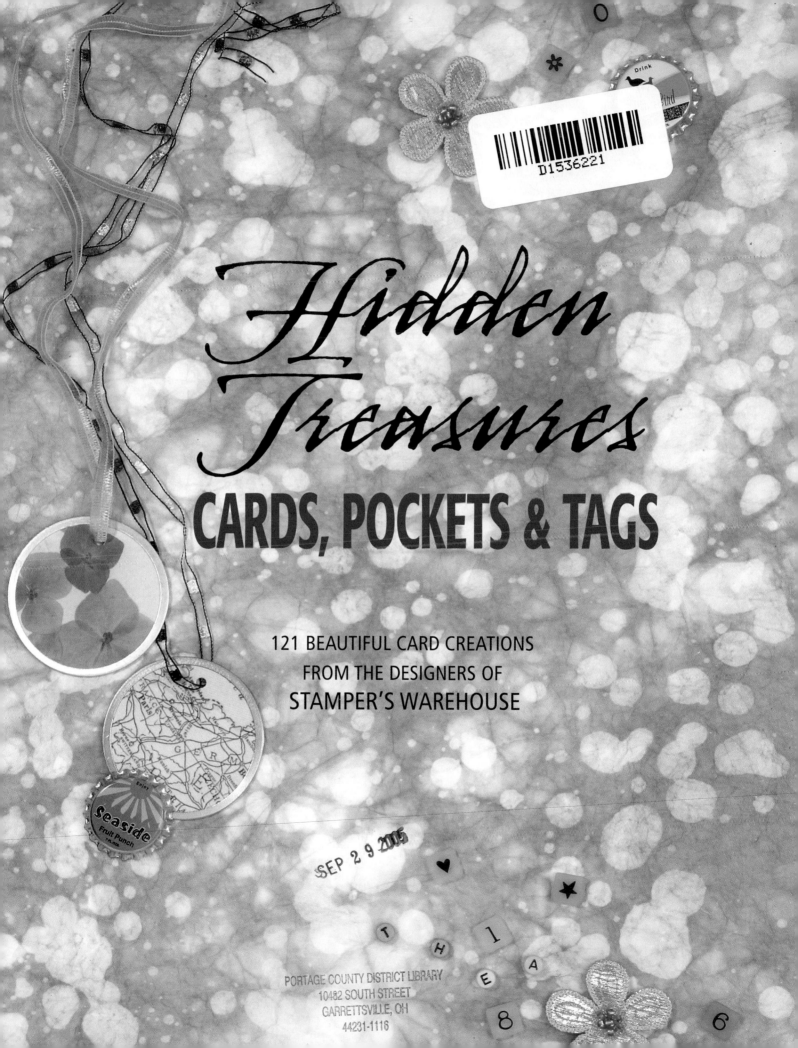

Hidden Treasures

CARDS, POCKETS & TAGS

121 BEAUTIFUL CARD CREATIONS
FROM THE DESIGNERS OF
STAMPER'S WAREHOUSE

SEP 2 9 2005

PORTAGE COUNTY DISTRICT LIBRARY
10482 SOUTH STREET
GARRETTSVILLE, OH
44231-1116

PRODUCED BY

Kooler Design Studio, Inc. • 399 Taylor Blvd., Ste. 104
 Pleasant Hill, CA 94523 • info@koolerdesign.com
 www.koolerdesign.com
Creative Director: Donna Kooler
Editor: Judy Swager
Project Manager, Book Designer, Photo Stylist: Basha Kooler
Book Designer: María Rodríguez
Writers: Basha Kooler, Sue Astroth, Project Designers
Photographer: Dianne Woods

Copyright © 2005 by Leisure Arts, Inc., 5701 Ranch Drive,
Little Rock, Arkansas 72223-9633.

All rights reserved. No part of this publication may be reproduced in any
form or by any means without permission in writing from the publisher.
Printed in the United States of America. The information in this book is
presented in good faith, however no warranty is given nor are results
guaranteed. Leisure Arts, Kooler Design Studio, Inc., and Donna Kooler
disclaim in any and all liability for untoward results. Not for commercial
reproduction.

We have made every effort to ensure that these instructions are accurate
and complete. We cannot, however, be responsible for human error,
typographical mistakes, or variations in individual work.

The designs in this book are protected by copyright; however, you may
make the designs for your personal use. This right is surpassed when
the designs are made by employees or sold commercially.

10 9 8 7 6 5 4 3 2 1

Library of Congress Cataloging-in-Publication Data
 Kooler, Donna
 Hidden Treasures Cards, Pockets & Tags
 "A Leisure Arts Publication"

 I S B N :   1 - 5 7 4 8 6 - 5 1 3 - 7

PUBLISHED BY

welcome

What luck, serendipity really, to have found a wellspring of creativity within the walls of Stamper's Warehouse, a paper crafters' paradise in Danville, California. *Scrapbooks & Beyond*, the first book of designs from the store's talented artists and teachers, was such an overwhelming success we just had to ask for a second book—this time focusing on cards, pockets and tags.

Phyllis Nelson, owner of Stamper's Warehouse, leads the lively band of artists who have created the unique designs in *Hidden Treasures, Cards, Pockets & Tags*. Once their collective minds started flowing, there was no end to the fabulous keepsakes they were to ultimately compose. As you turn the pages, you will find more than a hundred ideas to inspire you to create your own "card treasures" to share with family and friends.

It was a pleasure and privilege to work with this talented group.

Basha Kooler
Project Manager

PROJECT DESIGNERS

Sandi Allan
Sue Astroth
Connie Baldonado
Traci Bautista
Patty Carlson
Vanessa Cole
Debby DeBenedetti
Wilda Dupré
Diana Diaz
Stacie Enriquez
Jenn Gaub
Susan Gin
Krista Halligan
Linda Lavasani
Aileen Lew
Sandi Marr
Gail Martin
Phyllis Nelson
Barbara Osada
Janis Ramsden
Terrece Siddoway
Susan Thompson
Beckie Torgerson
Kathy Yee

Contents

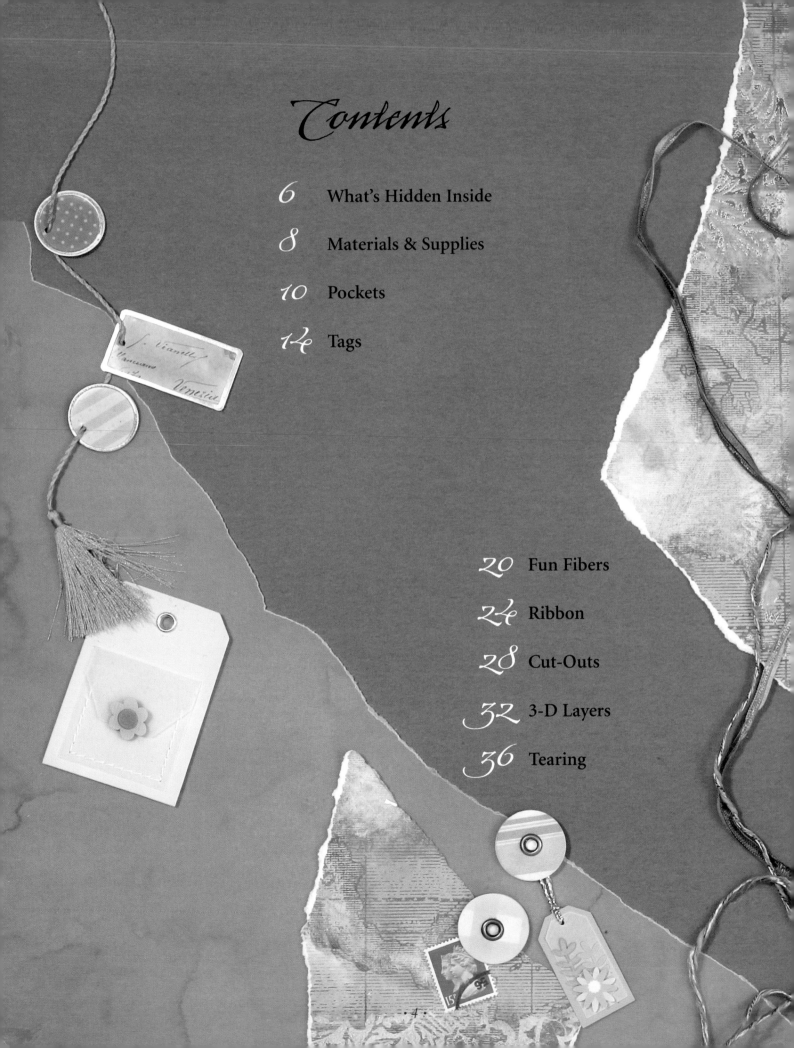

6   What's Hidden Inside

8   Materials & Supplies

10   Pockets

14   Tags

20   Fun Fibers

24   Ribbon

28   Cut-Outs

32   3-D Layers

36   Tearing

40 Beads

44 Buttons

46 Sewing & Weaving

50 Clay

54 Metal

58 Hand-tinting

62 The Artists

64 Resources

What's Hidden Inside

Making and sending a personal greeting is the perfect way to give a little of yourself and have lots of fun in the process. A wedding, a birthday, a graduation and even "just because" are all good reasons to send greeting cards. As children, many of us entered the world of art by creating cards for special friends and occasions.

In the "computer age" of instant messaging with abbreviated words and simple, disposable thoughts, there are few opportunities for communicating on a heartfelt, emotional level. How delightful it is to discover an envelope in the mailbox, personally addressed, in a script we know and love! The sense of recognition and anticipation that the envelope evokes far exceeds the jolt we feel when "You've Got Mail" is flashing on the computer screen. Hundreds of years ago, the poet John Donne observed that "letters mingle souls." How true! Nothing speaks to the heart like a card, designed and created by hand, especially for you.

All of us have experienced the joy of receiving a special greeting card, but there is also great satisfaction in sending a personal card to honor a friend, to celebrate an outstanding achievement, commemorate a milestone, or to share in the love a family feels for a new baby.

The scrapbook artist captures memories and emotions one page at a time. Once the project is complete, little bits of ribbon, pieces of decorative paper, and embellishments remain. They are just too pretty to toss or give away. What better way to use these remaining elements than by exploring the world of card-making?

Cool Stuff Inside

Have you visited your favorite stamp or scrapbook store recently? Scrapbook and stamping supplies complement a variety of artistic styles, enriching the card maker's repertoire. Stamper's Warehouse stocks beautiful paper in every color, pattern and texture imaginable; rubber stamps in a myriad of images, styles and sizes with coordinating sayings; alphabet sets to create your own sayings or thoughts; a full spectrum of inks paints and pens; brads, eyelets, and metals; decorative ribbons and fancy fibers to complete the look. Even computer programs are available to help design a special greeting. The artists featured here were inspired by all of these treasures.

Look around! Everything can be the catalyst for a card. Ideas may come from anywhere: fashion magazines, home decorating idea books, gift catalogs, a beautiful garden, an inspiring vista, a toddler's beaming face, the silhouette of a tree touching the sky. Your imagination is your only limit. Give yourself permission to experiment and enjoy the process without concern for the results. When the creative juices begin flowing, you'll find that you've produced something that expresses who you are and how you see the world.

Our featured artists appear on pages 62 and 63. As you thumb through this book, you'll see how these projects reflect the creators' individuality, interests and artistic style.

Great inspiration awaits you!

Materials & Supplies

decorative scissors

brushes

glue-dots

double-si

punches

pens & pencils

tools

papers

Distress Ink — peeled paint — Ranger

glazes

Bright Blue GLAZE
Water-Based Acrylic
Satin Finish
GOLDEN

adhesives

GORILLA GLUE

Pearl Ex Pigments

Zip Dry Paper Glue
FAST DRYING
GLUE FOR
PAPER ARTS

Diamond Glaze
Water-based
Dimensional
Adhesive

Crafter's Pick

antiquing glazes

Java Walnut

Pearl Pigments

FiberEtch Walnut tint

FiberEtch Walnut tint

JOURN

-John
dream
wak
an

metallic paint & powders

Pockets

What surprises are in store! Card artists love including little treasures in their creations that generate a sense of anticipation. Pockets and folds can reveal an unexpected gift like a bookmark or special message.

JUST FOR YOU
By Krista Halligan

Cardstock: metallic ivory, metallic light green
Floral patterned paper by Anna Griffin
Harlequin patterned paper
Ribbon
Honeydew Encore pigment ink pad
Clear embossing powder
Medium hole punch
Xyron with adhesive cartridge
Stamps by Anna Griffin from All Night Media

Directions: Cut ivory cardstock to $5^1/_2$" x $8^1/_2$". Fold in half to make $4^1/_4$" x $5^1/_2$" card. Cut a diagonal section off one side of folded card as seen in photo. Cut harlequin and floral paper $4^1/_4$" x $5^1/_2$". Cut floral paper in half on the diagonal (see photo). Open card and stamp pattern along diagonal edge using Encore Honeydew ink pad; emboss with clear embossing powder. Assemble card layers, placing harlequin paper on background and floral paper on front flap of card. Create layered tag, cutting outer piece to 3"x 5". Cut distressed layer to $2^3/_4$" x $4^3/_4$". Cut top layer to measure $2^1/_2$" x $4^1/_2$". Trim corners on one end and punch hole for tie. Stamp and emboss center design. Assemble layers and distress using Encore Honeydew ink pad. Run accent ribbon through Xyron and adhere to front panel of card. Place adhesive along the bottom, the left side, top left corner, and bottom right corner of front flap. Press down to adhere, creating a pocket for the tag.

BEACH BOOK
By Stacie Jo Enriquez

Background cardstock
"A Day at The Beach" 12" x 12" patterned cardstock by Autumn Leaves
Twill tape
Twine, 13" long
Embellishments: stickers, buttons, word charms, alphabets

Directions: Cut, fold and assemble 12" x 12" patterned paper per instructions on reverse of paper. Cut and mat photos on coordinating solid cardstock with adhesive. Attach charms, buttons, stickers, etc. as desired with adhesive. Center and adhere twine on the reverse side of last page. Center and adhere twill on top of twine. Wrap twine to front of card and tie bow.

POCKET FAN
By Linda Lavasani

Black cardstock
Lightweight cardboard
Washi paper and handmade textured
    black paper
Gold metallic vellum
Liquid paper adhesive
Small hole punch
Spine from a fan
Gold paint
Gold thread, beads, Asian charm and
    small black tassel
Double-sided tape

Directions: Cut a fan shape out of a 9" x 5" piece of lightweight cardboard (see photo). Cover with black handmade paper using liquid paper adhesive. Glue a piece of washi paper onto black cardstock. Trim it following the pattern of the paper along the top edge and the fan shape along the bottom. Attach this to the fan using double-sided tape along the bottom edge, but only halfway along the top edge to form a pocket. Punch a hole in the bottom of the fan and attach a tassel. Paint the fan spine gold. String the charm and beads onto the gold thread and sew onto the fan spine. Trim then slide into the pocket and tape in place. Make a small envelope using vellum and slip into the pocket.

SHE BE FIERCE
By Sandi Allan

Cardstock: patterned raspberry, pink, white
Girl overlay (acetate) by Memories Complete
Acrylic paints: medium fuchsia, white
Black and white checked ribbon,
    white ribbon
Silver flower embellishment and brad
Memories Complete cardstock stickers
Small hole punch

Directions: Cut a piece of pink cardstock, approximately 12" x 4³/₄". Fold in half. Brush edges with white paint. Cut raspberry patterned cardstock 11" x 3¹/₂". Fold in half. Cut the section of the overlay "Though she be but little.." to size. Paint with fuchsia on back of overlay, ensuring that paint covers only the words. Allow paint to dry. Tear white cardstock to fit behind overlay, following the shape of the words and glue to raspberry cardstock. To attach overlay to raspberry cardstock, punch three holes through the overlay and cardstock. Attach with checked ribbon. Tie a knot and trim. Attach silver flower embellishment on front of card, using a silver brad. Place the raspberry cardstock with the overlay and embellishments on the front of the pink cardstock. Line up the folds and glue down. Cut an 11" length of white ribbon. Paint the ends with fuchsia paint. Let dry. Wrap the ribbon around center of card and tie in front. Trim edges of ribbon with a diagonal cut. Cut a tag from pink cardstock 2³/₄" x 4". Attach sticker. Cut 4" lengths of checked and white ribbons. Paint the white ribbon with fuchsia paint. Punch hole and thread the ribbons through the hole. Knot and trim ends. Inside the card make a pocket for the tag. Cut raspberry cardstock 3¹/₂" x 2". Embellish with a sticker. Glue the inside edges of the pocket, ensuring that there is enough space to allow the tag to slide in.

POCKET INVITATION
By Krista Halligan

Cardstock: metallic gold
Patterned papers by K & Company
Metallic gold vellum
Embossing ink and turquoise tapestry
    embossing powder
Xyron with adhesive cartridge
Decorative scissors
Double-sided tape
Stamps by Anna Griffin from All Night Media

Directions: Cut gold cardstock to 7" x 11".
Cut red patterned paper to 7" x 10". Cut
blue patterned paper to 7" x 6$^1/_2$". Run red
and blue layers through Xyron machine.
Center red layer on gold cardstock and
adhere to outside of card. On inside, score 3"
from the bottom of the card. Fold bottom up.
Place blue patterned paper on inside of card,
beginning at the bottom fold line and adhere.
Score entire piece 3" from top and fold top
down. Trim gold edges using decorative scissors. Create pocket by sealing edges of bottom flap with double-sided tape. Cut inside
gold card to 4" x 6". Cut blue layer 3$^3/_4$" x
5$^3/_4$". For inside card, cut red layer 3$^1/_2$"x 5
$^1/_2$". Cut gold layer 3$^1/_4$" x 5$^1/_4$". Assemble
layers and slide into pocket. Cut gold flap to
3$^1/_4$" square. Cut blue layer to 3" square.
Cut gold layer to 2$^3/_4$" square. Stamp image
using embossing ink and emboss with
turquoise tapestry embossing powder.
Secure flap to top only, using double-sided
tape.

HIDDEN SECRETS CD TIN
By Beckie Torgerson

Themed stamps for ocean or travel
CD tin
Metal primer
Acrylic paints: light green, cream, rose,
    soft yellow
Graphite Black Brilliance ink pad
Embellishments: small sea shells, small glass
    bottle, domino, letter tiles, flat marble,
    woven ribbon, small beads,
    decorative sand
Perfect Paper Adhesive (PPA) by USArtQuest
White tissue paper
Colored pencils
Metal adhesive
Adirondack pens
Acrylic spray sealer

Directions: Paint interior and exterior of CD tin
with metal primer. Apply thin coat of base color to
tin. Streak with other colors using a soft brush.
Let dry thoroughly. Stamp some of the stamp
images on tissue paper. Color with colored pencils. Cut out images close to outside lines. Apply
images to CD tin using PPA. Apply a top coat of
PPA over images to seal. Stamp other images
directly on CD tin using Brilliance Ink. Let dry
thoroughly or heat set. (Note: If heat is too
intense, paint will bubble). Glue on other embellishments and sand.

Domino:

Stamp image with Black Brilliance Ink. Re-ink
stamp and stamp domino edges to appear as
though the design is wrapping around the domino. Color using Adirondack pens. Seal with acrylic
spray sealer. Glue in place.

FAN CARD
By Susan Thompson

Cardstock: red, tan
Patterned paper to coordinate with cardstock
Fan sticker or image
Tassel
Brad
Raffia
Xyron machine with adhesive cartridge
Small hole punch
Decorative scissors

Directions: Cut cardstock $8^1/2$" x $5^1/2$". Cut a piece of coordinating paper $5^1/4$" x $8^1/4$" and another $5^1/4$" x $3^3/4$". Run the large piece of coordinating paper through the Xyron machine. Adhere to one side of the cardstock. Fold the card in half with the patterned paper to the inside. Apply adhesive to the smaller coordinating paper. Adhere to card front. Fold the top and bottom right corners to meet each other and create a pocket. Punch a small hole in each of the corners and thread raffia through holes. Tie into a small bow. Adhere fan image to tan cardstock and trim $1/4$" from edge, using decorative scissors. Punch hole at bottom of fan and insert brad. Hang tassel from brad and slide into pocket.

WITCH POCKET CARD
By Sue Astroth

Two sheets gray-black metallic cardstock
One sheet black textured cardstock
One sheet copper metallic cardstock
Philadelphia lower case "w" stencil by Making
    Memories
$5/8$" black rayon ribbon, 20" long
Witch charm and jump ring
Eye pin (a jewelry finding)
Alphabet stamps
Witch hat stamp by Rubber Stamps of America
White pigment ink
Acrylic paints: black, silver metallic
Black thread and sewing machine
Vintage photo
1" and $1/2$" circle punches

Directions: Carefully pop out the "w" in the letter stencil and paint black. Paint the stencil background metallic silver. Let dry. Cut two $5^3/4$" x $6^1/4$" pieces gray-black cardstock. Tear away $1^1/2$" on one piece; this becomes the top. Lay the torn piece on top of the full piece, lining up at the bottom. Using the presser foot as a sewing guide, sew together along three sides, leaving the torn edge open. Cut a 4" x $4^1/2$" piece of copper cardstock. Wrap twice with rayon ribbon and tie knot on front. Adhere copper cardstock to pocket card just inside stitching lines. Place "w" back into stencil background. With a dry brush, add a little black paint to the background as a highlight. Let dry. Stamp "icked" and "itch" with white ink on scraps of gray cardstock. Trim and adhere to card. Glue "w" stencil to card. Attach charm to eye pin with jump ring. Pin into knot. For the tag, cut a $5^1/2$" x $4^1/4$" piece of black cardstock. Punch a $1/2$-inch circle at one end of the black cardstock. Use the two circle punches to make a reinforcement from the copper cardstock. Stamp witch hat on copper cardstock and cut out. Mat the photo with gray cardstock. Adhere reinforcement, photo and hat to tag. Thread black ribbon through hole and tie with slip knot.

Tags

They aren't just for packages anymore. From ornate angels to elegant Asian motifs, tags, fluttering like leaves in the wind, are everywhere. Many die-cut systems and punches are available for making tags. With a quick punch, a variety of shapes and sizes are ready to use.

dreams do come ♡ true

ANGEL PAPER DOLL TAGS
By Traci Bautista

Natural-colored cardstock
Handmade and patterned papers
Ribbon
Silk flower leaves
Fibers, tulle
Assorted stamps
Ink pad
Glitter gel pen

Directions: Create a doll shape or use a template. Trace twice on cardstock. Cut out doll shapes. Stamp various stamps on cardstock. Tear or cut assorted papers into small pieces. Glue collage pieces and words on doll. Adhere silk flowers on paper doll. Embellish with fibers and wrap with tulle. Glue silk flower leaves to back of cardstock to create wings. Glue ribbon onto top. Glue second doll shape to the back of paper doll. Draw designs, such as swirls and dots, with a glitter gel pen.

POSTAGE ART
By Ailene Lew

Cardstock: green marbled, gold, white
Black ink pad by Memories
Memories Ink pads: Soft Rose, Soft Yellow, Soft Lavender, Soft Sage.
Postage Art stamp by Hero Arts
Skyland Bookmark stamp by Hero Arts
Leaves and Patterns stamp by Hero Arts
Colored pencils
Silk ribbons and gold cord
Sponge
Deckle-edge scissors
Mounting tape

Directions: Stamp images on white cardstock using a black ink pad. Sponge soft colors from ink pads onto stamped images. Using gold, brown and yellow colored pencils, shade woman's hair on the Postage Art image and maple leaves on the other two images. Cut out images; use deckle-edge scissors on Postage Art. Adhere to gold cardstock and cut around edges, leaving a 1/16" border. Punch hole in tag and tie ribbons and cord. Adhere tag to green marbled card. Using one layer of mounting tape, adhere Postage Art image. Using two layers of mounting tape, attach leaves and pattern image.

GEISHA TAG CARD
By Kathy Yee

Cardstock : black, gold, red
Assorted Asian stamps
Chinese coin set stamps by A Stamp in the Hand
Metallic gold ink pad
Black dye-based ink pad
Watercolor markers
Small merchandise tag
Gold cord
Krylon gold pen
1/8" circle punch
Foam mounting tape

Directions: Make red tag with a $1^7/8$" x $3^1/2$" piece red cardstock. Stamp a geisha with black dye-based ink on the tag. Stamp the coins and small Asian stamps randomly around the geisha with gold ink. Outline the edges of the red tag using the Krylon gold pen. Remove the string from the merchandise tag. Re-ink the geisha stamp with black ink and lay it rubber side up. Lay the merchandise tag over the face of the geisha. Pat lightly and then carefully lift the tag off the stamp. Heat set ink. Color the merchandise tag with watercolor markers. Outline the edge of merchandise tag with a Krylon gold pen. Mount the merchandise tag over the face of the geisha using foam mounting tape. Punch a hole in the red tag through the hole of the merchandise tag. Tie the gold cord through the two tags and tie a knot. Trim the cord. Stamp the coin stamps randomly on the left side of the red cardstock in gold and black ink. Stamp Asian writing and character stamp on the right side in gold and black. Mount the gold cardstock to the black card. Mount the red cardstock to the gold. Mount the red tag at the top using foam mounting tape.

ALPHA CARD
By Barbara Osada

Cardstock: red, tan, black, navy, gray, white
Block head stamp by Leavenworth Jackson
Art, numerals by Limited Edition
Key, watch by Above the Mark
Black, brown dye-based ink pads
Gold embossing powder
Gold threads
Punches

Directions: Stamp the background figures using a brown ink pad on a red folded card, measuring $4^1/4$" x $5^1/2$". On navy cardstock, emboss the alphabet stamp with clear embossing ink and gold embossing powder. Emboss the word "Art" on the bottom of the black cardstock. Stamp numbers with black ink on the tan cardstock. Layer navy, black, and tan cardstock as shown. Punch hole at top center. On scrap paper, stamp the clock and block head image with black ink. Emboss the key image with gold embossing powder. Cut out each of these and treat them like tags. Make the black reinforcement using two punches and adhere. Thread gold threads through hole at top. Insert gold threads through reinforced hole. Attach stamped layers with hanging tags.

VISION
By Linda Lavasani

Copper metallic cardstock
Metallic gold textured paper
Copper paper
Black patterned paper
Word stamp
Small piece of mica
Photocopy of Renaissance woman
Gold leaf and Duo adhesive
    By USArtQuest
Diamond Glaze by JudiKins
Black pigment ink
Black Diamond embossing powder by Judikins
Embellishments: key, key hole, 2 brads, pieces of
    glass, ribbon

Directions: Cut copper metallic cardstock in the shape of a tag. Along the bottom edge, stamp word in black pigment ink and emboss using Black Diamond embossing powder. Cut the gold textured paper to size, then cut and tear the black cardstock and layer onto the copper piece. Tear and layer sections from the patterned paper. Tear the photocopy of the woman so that it is a little larger than the piece of mica, but allowing some of the mica to show. Use Duo adhesive to coat the back side of the mica. When dry and tacky, lay the photocopy on the mica, fill in the clear sections with gold leaf, then trim and adhere to the tag. Attach the keyhole using brads. Adhere the key and glass bits with Diamond Glaze. Punch a hole in the tag; thread ribbon through the hole and head of key. Knot ribbon.

ASIAN TAGS ON TWIG
By Barbara Osada

Cardstock: tan, black, two shades of red
Tags
Ink pads: black, brown, olive, taupe, rust
Gold embossing powder
Assorted Asian stamps
22-gauge gold wire
Twig
Tacky glue

Directions: Color each of the tags with the various ink pads, using the direct-to-paper technique. Stamp the Asian images with coordinating colors. Add the calligraphy with black ink. String the tags together using the gold wire and tie to the twig. Layer the background red cardstock on black cardstock and a tan card. Stamp more calligraphy in black for the background. Emboss a yin-yang symbol with gold embossing powder at the lower corner. Attach twig and tags with tacky glue.

BLACK & WHITE CLOCKS
By Barbara Osada

Cardstock: black, white
Black & white checked paper
Words by Inkadinkado
Watch & clock stamps by Above the Mark
Text stamp
Small tag
Pigment ink pads: black, gold, copper, white
Ink pads: rust, ochre
Gold embossing powder
Gold photo corners
Gold metallic marker
Mounting tape

Directions: Stamp a variety of watches and clocks on black cardstock with white, gold and copper pigment inks. When dry, stamp the quote and emboss with gold embossing powder. Add the gold photo corners and draw lines, using a gold metallic marker. Position on the black and white layered card. Emboss the watch with black pigment ink and gold embossing powder. Trim and color with the ochre and brown ink pads for an aged look. On the small tag, color with a rust ink pad and stamp additional watch images. Tie the tag with gold thread and attach to the clock. Add dimension by applying foam tape to the clock and adhere to card.

ASIAN COIN TAG
By Barbara Osada

Cardstock: maroon, red, black
Handmade paper
Tag
Stamps
Walnut ink
Ink pads: black, brown, rust
Gold craft wire
Asian coins
Twigs & raffia
Glue Dots

Directions: Paint the tag with walnut ink. Stamp a variety of Asian images in black, rust and brown inks. Add a scrap of red cardstock to the center. Thread the Asian coins with raffia, inserting twigs. Secure with glue dots. Coil the gold wire around a pencil and add an embellishment tag to the end. Finish the tag with an edge of black cardstock. Adhere handmade paper to the maroon card and attach the tag.

LAUGHTER POCKET TAG
By Debby DeBenedetti

Assorted cardstock
Skeleton leaf
Ribbon charm
Variety of embellishments
Ribbon or fiber
Envelope & tag templates

Directions: Cut a variety of tag shapes and sizes from cardstock. Stamp message or attach photo to one tag. Use a variety of techniques on a few of the tags, i.e., sand, emboss, distress, stamp, etc. Embellish remaining tags. Using envelope template, cut one envelope from cardstock. Fold all flaps, except top flap. Secure in place with adhesive, forming a pocket. Cut a liner for the envelope using the same template. Trim off side and bottom flaps so that liner slides into pocket. Set aside one small tag. Attach remaining tags with ribbons and fibers. Insert in pocket. Attach skeleton leaf to front of pocket. Wrap ribbons around pocket. Thread ribbon tails through ribbon charm so they overlap. Adhere to front of pocket. Insert another ribbon through remaining tag and through corner of charm, so tag dangles from charm. Attach additional embellishments to front of pocket.

WEDDING WISHES
By Debby DeBenedetti

Cardstock
Tag template
Quotes on marriage
Microbeads
Small alphabet stamps
Ribbon or fiber, approx.. 10" long
Fabric ink pad
Acrylic bubbles
Dye-based ink pad
Variety of embellishments
Sticker-making machine, such as Xyron
Small circle punch, approx.. $^{1}/_{2}$" – $^{3}/_{4}$"

Directions: Print quotes on cardstock. Center quote on tag template and cut out tag shape around quote, leaving enough room for embellishments. Distress tag by rubbing edge of tag over dye-based ink pad. Stamp bride's and groom's initials on ribbon several times. Set ribbon aside. Spread glue on upper left corner of tag and dip in beads. Allow to dry. Print couple's names on cardstock, using a computer. Be certain font is small enough to fit inside the acrylic bubble. Punch out names with circle punch. Place acrylic bubble on punched-out circles. Adhere to tag. Using stickers and various coordinating embellishments, embellish lower right corner of tag. Tie ribbon through tag hole.

A happy marriage has in it all the pleasures of FRIENDSHIP, all the ENJOYMENTS of sense and reason, and indeed, all the sweets of life.
-Anonymous

A happy marriage is the world's best bargain.
-O.A. Battista

L TAG
By Sandi Allan

Cardstock: lavender, pink
Raspberry print two-sided cardstock
Silver brads
White sheer ribbon
Silver alphabet letter embellishment with eye
1/8" hole punch

Directions: Fold lavender cardstock in half so that the folded card measures 4 1/2" x 8". Cut a raspberry strip measuring 3 1/2" x 3". Tear edge off the 3" side, keeping close to the edge. Fold strip in half. Glue pink cardstock to the back of the torn edge so that it forms a flap. Center and glue flapped card to the front of the lavender card about 1/2" down from the top. Make a lavender tag 2 1/4" x 4 1/2". Punch a hole at the top and thread sheer ribbon and alphabet letter through. Tie a knot and trim excess. Make a pocket for the tag by cutting raspberry cardstock 1" x 3". Glue the edges down to the pink cardstock, ensuring that the tag can slide through the back. Attach three silver brads to bottom of pink strip. Glue silver heart embellishment to top of flap. Using the light side of raspberry paper, cut a strip 4 1/2" x 3". Tear the widest edge, leaving a white edge. Glue to lavender cardstock, lining up with bottom of card. Punch two small holes on bottom right side. Thread sheer ribbon through each hole and knot; trim. Center the second piece of pink cardstock inside the card and adhere.

HOLIDAY TAGS
By Traci Bautista

Cardstock
Acrylic paint & ink
Glitter, beads, crystals, coins
Metal foil tape
Eyelets
Brads
Microbeads
Stamps
Gel pen
Diamond Glaze
Small bell
Multi-color metallic ink pad

Directions:

"Joy" Tag
Paint cardstock with acrylic paint. Cut tag shapes from cardstock. Write "joy" with a gel pen. Cut and attach a strip of tacky tape. Cover with glitter and microbeads then adhere the crystal. Wrap fibers to create hang tag and add bell.

Snowflake Tag
Cut out two tag shapes from cardstock, one each red and of cream. Stamp snowflakes on red cardstock with multi-color metallic ink pad. Tear red cardstock and adhere on top of first tag shape. Emboss design into metal foil tape and adhere to tag. Write "happy holidays" with a gel pen. Add Christmas tree brad and tie with twine.

Peace Tag
Cut out tag shape from cardstock. Tear bottom of cardstock. Swipe multi-color metallic ink pad across tag. Write "Peace" on tag with a gel pen. Punch a hole and add a Christmas tree brad. Set an eyelet into top hole and attach fibers to create hang tag.

Dimensional Collage Tag
Cut out tag shape from cardstock and adhere torn handmade papers. Paint Diamond Glaze onto the tag with a brush. Sprinkle on glitter. Paint lines with an eyedropper of acrylic ink. Sprinkle glitter flakes and microbeads on center of card. Apply Diamond Glaze over glitters to set in place. Attach a Chinese coin.

"Joy" Bead Tag
Paint cardstock with acrylic paint. Cut tag shapes from cardstock. Cut and apply a strip of tacky tape. Cover with microbeads. Adhere letter beads spelling "JOY." Tie a ribbon to create hang tag.

PASTEL HEART WITH TAG
By Barbara Osada

Cardstock: lavender, olive, light green, white
Black dye-based ink pad
Pigment ink pads: turquoise, olive, yellow, pink, purple
Heart stamp by Hero Arts
Swirl stamp
Small tag
Silver eyelet and setting tools
Hot pink marker
Silver thread

Directions: Mount a piece of light green cardstock to the lavender card. Using the direct-to-paper technique, apply various colored pigment inks to a piece of white cardstock and the small tag. With a black dye-based ink pad, stamp the heart image. Stamp the musical swirl on the small tag. Add highlights to the heart image with a hot pink marker. Complete with the silver eyelet and string the tag with silver thread. Edge the image with olive cardstock and adhere to card.

BY THE NUMBERS
By Linda Lavasani

Cardstock: black, red
Patterned paper by 7gypsies
Alphabet rub-ons by Making Memories
Various "number" elements: matchbook with phone number written inside, ticket stub, postage stamp, foreign currency, old recipe card, image of measuring tape, pocket watch, dice, domino, price tag, etc.
Fibers and ribbon

Directions: Cut black cardstock for the back of the tag. Adhere the measuring tape down the right side and the rub-ons down the left side. Use the red cardstock to make two pockets (cut straight on the left side and tear unevenly on the right side). Make the top pocket in the same manner, using the patterned paper. Add elements and embellish with fibers and ribbon.

Fun Fibers

With styles like eyelash, fur and boa, novelty and natural fibers definitely add a sense of warmth, texture and whimsy to your greetings. Wrap fibers around a special element or string them with beads as a tactile design accent.

SCREEN CARD
By Debby DeBenedetti

Assorted cardstock
Screening from hardware store, approx..
   $3^1/2$" x $8^1/2$"
Glue Dots
Ribbon, fibers
Embellishments
$1/8$" hole punch
Transparency film
Message stamp and ink pad

Directions: Cut a sheet of cardstock 8" x $9^3/8$". Fold in half, lengthwise. Using a computer, print selected quotes or messages pertaining to the theme of the card on the transparency film. Trim around quotes in various rectangular shapes. Layer quotes on various cardstock. Trim cardstock to size of transparencies. Set transparency/cardstock units aside. Trim a sheet of patterned cardstock to $1^1/2$" x 8 $1/4$". Punch holes approximately $1/2$" from top and bottom edges. Embellish cardstock with key, charm, etc. Insert brads into punched holes and secure vertically to screening. Secure transparency/cardstock units to screening, using staples, brads, safety pins, etc. Secure screening to folded cardstock with glue dots. Position ribbon on inside and outside of fold and knot at top of card.

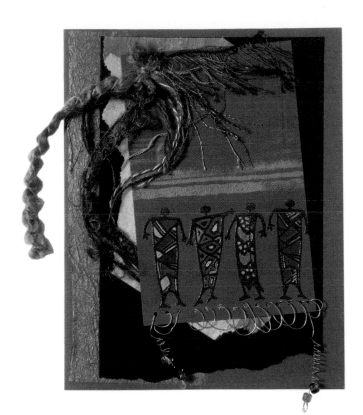

AFRICAN FIGURES

By Barbara Osada

Cardstock: brown, black, maroon
Gold & metallic blue-gray handmade papers
Ethnic stamp by M.J. Barber
Ink pads: black, gold
Gold and black embossing powder
28-gauge gold wire
Markers, metallic gel pens
Beads, fibers

Directions: Layer the torn metallic blue-gray, black and gold papers on a brown folded card. Emboss the African figures with black pigment ink and black embossing powder on maroon cardstock. Color with markers and metallic gel pens. Add the stripes with gold pigment ink and gold embossing powder. Punch a row of holes at the bottom and loop the gold wire. Add beads to each end. Adhere fibers in top left corner, then adhere maroon cardstock to card catching loose ends of fibers.

SKELETON LEAF CARD

By Barbara Osada

Sage cardstock
Patterned paper
Washi paper
Vellum with sparkles
Scraps of mulberry, metallic & handmade
  papers
Skeleton leaf
Gold eyelets and setting tools
Paper crimper
Fibers

Directions: Add the patterned paper to a sage card. Glue a narrow piece of washi paper on the right side. Cut an irregular piece of the sparkle vellum for the overlay. Crimp the strip of metallic paper and set with gold eyelets. Layer the remaining mulberry and handmade paper scraps before adding the skeleton leaf and fibers.

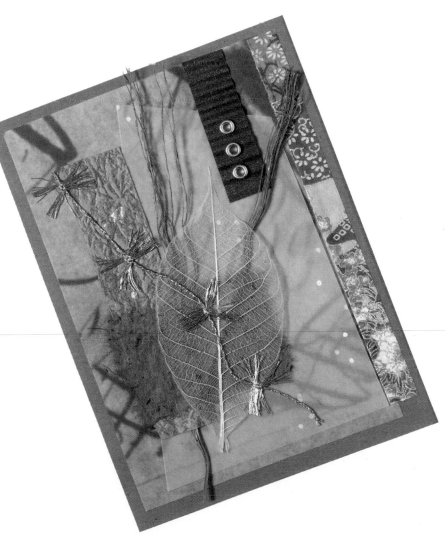

BLUE SUN
By Barbara Osada

Cardstock: turquoise, dark & medium
 blue, black
Purple vellum
Blue mulberry paper
Sun stamp by Leavenworth Jackson
Assorted background and word stamps
Ink pads: black, lapis, white
Embossing powders: gold, silver, clear
Fibers
Foam tape

Directions: Tear mulberry paper and attach to turquoise card. Stamp cloud image with white ink on dark blue cardstock. Emboss leaf image with lapis pigment ink and clear embossing powder on medium blue cardstock. Stamp some text with black ink. On a strip of purple vellum, emboss "believe" with gold embossing powder. Assemble and adhere all layers as shown. Stamp the sun on black cardstock using clear embossing ink and emboss with silver embossing powder. Trim and attach with foam tape. Finish by adhering a group of fibers that is knotted on both ends and adhere knots to card as shown.

PURPLE TRI-FOLD CARD
By Barbara Osada

Cardstock: purple, turquoise, navy
Purple vellum
Blue mulberry paper
Blossom stamps by Curtis Uyeda
Wheat stamp by Hanko Designs
Ink pads: brown, turquoise
Bronze Pearl-Ex powder
Gold embossing powder
Twig, fibers
Hole punch
Tacky glue

Directions: Score the purple cardstock $2^1/2$" from one short end. Score 2" from other end. Fold to make the tri-fold base card. Cut purple vellum for the overlay and score as above. Lightly glue ends with a glue stick to hold in place. Tear a strip of blue mulberry paper and adhere along center of card. On navy cardstock, emboss blossom image with clear embossing ink and gold embossing powder. Lightly rub edges with a brown ink pad to age and darken. On turquoise cardstock, emboss the wheat image with gold. Age with the turquoise ink pad. Add highlights with the bronze Pearl-Ex. Tie fibers around the twig and attach with tacky glue. Wrap around card. On inside flap, punch hole close to edge at center. Thread fibers through, add tacky glue to secure. Trim fibers as desired.

WORDS TO LIVE BY
By Linda Lavasani

Cardstock: slightly textured golden mustard,
   gold metallic moiré, white glossy
Stamps: Marble Cube by Stampendous,
   Zoroastrian symbol
Piece of mica
Brown ink & clear embossing ink
Gold detail embossing powder
Krylon gold pen
2 brads and metal spacer beads
Alcohol inks: red pepper, butterscotch,
   espresso
Alcohol blending solution
Round craft stick, 6" long
Double-sided tape
Japanese screw punch
Assorted fibers and ribbons

Directions: Color white glossy paper using
alcohol inks and blender. When dry, the text
can be printed directly on the paper by computer. (The text placement is determined by
the size and shape of the mica.) Trim and
layer on the gold paper. Cut the golden mustard cardstock to 4³/4" x 11" for back.
Stamp with the marble cube in brown ink.
Fold back the left edge about 2". Use a craft
knife to cut out three ¹/2" x ¹/2" sections
along the fold line. Position the craft stick and
secure the fold with double sided tape on the
reverse. Center gold/marbled piece on back
piece and adhere. On the front side of the
mica, stamp the symbol in clear embossing
ink; sprinkle on gold detail embossing powder and heat. On the reverse side of the
mica, color in the image using the gold pen.
Punch two holes through the mica and
papers using the screw punch and attach
with brads and spacer beads. (The spacer
beads are under the mica.) Layer this onto
the back piece. Embellish the craft stick with
assorted fibers and ribbons.

NAUTILUS FERN
By Barbara Osada

Black cardstock
Nautilus stencil by Dreamweaver
Botanical paper
Handmade silver paper
Text stamp
Dye-based ink pads: black, taupe
Translucent embossing paste
Brilliant Gold Pearl -Ex powder
Palette knife
Hole punch
Twig, fibers

Directions: Stamp the text with black ink on
a piece of botanical paper. Using the direct-to
paper technique, add some taupe ink next to
the text. Attach to a black folded card. Stencil
the nautilus on black cardstock using the
translucent embossing paste and a pinch of
Brilliant Gold Pearl-Ex powder. Spread with a
palette knife, dry completely and trim. Tear a
piece of silver handmade paper, punch holes
for the twig and insert as shown. Tie fibers
around twig and glue in place. Glue silver
paper to card.

Ribbon

Not just for making pretty bows anymore, ribbon is being sewn, glued, knotted, tied, painted, and even stamped with messages to tie together paper creations. A bit of ribbon can be just the thing to add a final flourish and softer look to a project.

QUEEN POCKET CARD
By Sue Astroth

Green-gold metallic cardstock
Gold metallic paper
Cardstock scraps: dark green, red
Black maruyama mesh
Philadelphia lower case "q" stencil by
    Making Memories
1" gold metal-rimmed tag
Crown charm
$7/8$" gold ribbon, 20" long
Various alphabet stamps
Queen stamp by Stampland
Metallic gold pigment ink
Solvent-based black ink
Small gold safety pin
$1/8$" green ribbon
Gold pen
Acrylic paint: green, metallic gold
Fleur-de-lis and gold crown embellishments
Sewing machine and green thread
$1/2$" & 1" circle punches
Small heart punch

Directions: Assemble pocket in same way as Girley Girl card at left except paint the letter gold with green background and use green-gold cardstock. Cut a 4" x $4^1/2$" piece of gold cardstock. Cut a 4" x $4^1/2$" piece of black maruyama, cutting between fibers. Fray edges by pulling away one or two threads. Lay on gold cardstock. Wrap gold ribbon twice around maruyama/gold cardstock and tie a knot on front. Center and glue the maruyama/gold cardstock to top of pocket card, just inside the stitching lines. Punch circle of green cardstock and glue in center of gold metal-rimmed tag. Punch hole at top. Tie tag to gold safety pin with green ribbon. Pin safety pin to back of gold knot. Using foam tape, adhere gold crown to metal-rimmed tag. Place "q" back into stencil background. Using gold pigment ink, stamp "the" on the stencil vertically in the upper left corner. On scrap of green cardstock, stamp "ueen" with the larger alphabet and gold pigment ink. Cut a 2" x $2^1/2$" piece of green-gold cardstock. Highlight the edge with the gold pen. Arrange and glue "q", gold edge cardstock and "ueen" just above gold ribbon on card. Punch small heart from red cardstock and glue to stencil above gold ribbon knot. For the tag, cut a $4^1/4$" x $5^1/2$" piece of green-gold cardstock. Make reinforcement using gold cardstock and two punches. Punch a $1/2$-inch circle at the top of the green tag. Glue the reinforcement around the hole. Attach the sheer green ribbon to the tag with a slipknot. Cut a piece of gold cardstock $2^3/4$" x 3". Using solvent ink, stamp queen image, centering face on gold cardstock. From green cardstock, cut a 3" x $3^1/4$" piece to mat the queen. Glue to tag.

GIRLEY GIRL CARD
By Sue Astroth

Cardstock: lime green, violet
Decorative paper
Violet checked ribbon, 1 yard
Philadelphia lowercase "g" stencil by Making
    Memories
Acrylic paint: lime green
Happy Birthday & alphabet stamps
Green dye-based ink pad
2 flower charms
Pink safety pin
Lavender brad
Sewing machine and lime green thread
$1/2$" & 1" circle punches

Directions: Carefully pop out the "g" in the letter stencil and paint lime green. Paint the stencil background pink. Let dry. Cut two $5^3/4$" x $6^1/4$" pieces lime green cardstock. Tear away $1^1/2$" on one piece; this becomes the top. Lay the torn piece on top of the full piece, lining up at bottom. Sew together along three sides, leaving the torn edge open and using machine foot as a sewing guide. Cut a $4^1/2$" x $4^1/4$" piece of decorative paper. Mat with violet cardstock. Wrap twice with checked ribbon and tie knot on front. Glue to front of pocket card. Using green dye-based ink, stamp "irley", "irl" and "Happy Birthday" on scraps of green cardstock. Place "g" back into stencil background. Mat the "g" stencil with violet cardstock. Glue "g", "irley" and "irl" on front of card. Attach flower charm to safety pin with jump ring. Pin to knot in ribbon. Cut a $5^1/2$" x $4^1/4$" piece of violet cardstock for tag. Make large reinforcement accent for the tag using two punches. Adhere reinforcement and "happy birthday" to front of tag. Attach flower charm to upper left corner with brad. Using a slip knot, tie ribbon to top of tag.

PEAR POCKET CARD
By Sue Astroth

Cardstock: metallic copper, dark green,
   cream, copper
Patterned patina paper
$1^1/4$" copper-trimmed aqua ribbon, $3/4$ yard
Pear charm and jump ring
Eyelet pin
Copper cord, $1/2$ yard
Aspen leaf stamp by Rubber Stampede
Oak leaf stamp by A Stamp in the Hand
Copper-colored thread and sewing machine
Clear embossing ink pad and copper emboss-
   ing powder
$1/2$" & 1" circle punches

Directions: Assemble pocket in same way as
Girley Girl card at left except use metallic
copper cardstock. Cut a $5^1/4$" x $4^3/4$" piece
of green cardstock. Layer a 5" x $4^1/2$" piece
of patina paper on top and glue to front of
pocket. Wrap ribbon around pocket, tie into a
bow, and trim ends. On cream cardstock,
Stamp two leaves on cream cardstock using
embossing ink and emboss with copper
embossing powder. Cut out close to
embossed outline. Cut $1^5/8$" oval from scraps
of green and copper cardstock. Trim $1/16$" off
green oval and glue to copper oval. Adhere
pear charm. Attach jump ring to top of tag
and eyelet pin. Pin into center of bow. Glue
the long leaf to the right of the pear tag,
tucking the stem under the ribbon. For the
large tag, cut $3^3/4$" x $5^1/8$" from green cardstock. Punch a $1/2$" circle at the top of the
green tag. Use the two circle punches to
make a reinforcement from the patina paper.
Glue around the hole. Tie the copper cording
to the tag with a slipknot. Glue aspen leaf to
center of tag. On computer, generate holiday
wish, print, cut out, and glue just at the bottom of stem.

BABY CARD
By Susan Gin and Janis Ramsden

Cardstock: pink, green, white
Pastel diamond print paper
Pink pigment ink pad
Pastel embossing powder by JudiKins
Baby stamp by Paper Inspirations
Pink ribbon: sheer, polka dot, grosgrain
Plastic pink mini pacifier
Pink wire

Directions: Cut a square pink card and layer
with green cardstock and diamond print
paper. Stamp and emboss baby stamp with
pink pigment ink and pastel embossing powder on a square of white cardstock emulating
a baby block. Adhere pink grosgrain ribbon
across top and bottom edge of block. Make a
bow using three ribbons of equal length and
wire a plastic pacifier around the bow. Center
bow at top of block and adhere.

POSTCARD ON BLACK & WHITE
By Barbara Osada

Cardstock: white, brown
Black & white check, map, measuring tape
**   patterned paper**
Index card
Text stamp by Inkadinkado
Assorted stamps
Ink pads: black, ochre, taupe, rust
Black & white dotted ribbon

Directions: Layer the black and white paper, map, and measuring tape patterned paper on a large white card. Color the index card with ochre and taupe ink pads, using the direct-to-paper technique. Stamp the images and adhere handmade paper at corners. Add a faux postage stamp. Glue dotted ribbon on left side as shown. Adhere postcard to backing. Add a thin strip of brown cardstock across lower right corner.

PINK & RED TOILE LOVERS
By Krista Halligan

Cardstock: metallic red, metallic fuchsia,
    white parchment
$1^1/2$" pink/orange striped ribbon, 15" long
Warm red chalk ink by Clearsnap
Toile stamps by All Night Media
Pop-Up Glue Dots

Directions: Cut red cardstock to make a 5"
x 7" folded card. Cut fuchsia layer to $4^3/4$"x
$6^3/4$". Cut red layer to $4^1/4$" x $3^3/4$". Cut
smaller fuchsia layer 4" x $3^1/2$". Stamp
image in red chalk ink on white parchment.
Heat set. Trim to $3^3/4$" x $3^1/4$". Adhere last
three layers. Adhere large fuchsia piece to red
card. Fold ribbon in half and adhere with glue
dots; trim ends. Adhere assembled stamped
image on top of ribbon using pop-up glue
dots.

SYMPATHY CARD
By Krista Halligan

Cardstock: Metallic blue, metallic green
1" iridescent blue-green ribbon, 12" long
Clear embossing powder
Brilliance Midnight ink
Stamps by Anna Griffin from All Night Media
Pop-Up Glue Dots

Directions: Cut blue card to $4^1/4$" x $5^1/2$".
Cut green layer to 4"x $5^1/4$". Cut blue layer
to $3^1/2$" x $3^1/2$". Cut green layer to $3^1/4$" x
3". Stamp background image on larger green
layer in Midnight ink. Emboss in clear and
trim to edge of design. Stamp image and
words on small green layer with Midnight
ink. Emboss with clear powder. Attach background image to card. Fold ribbon in half and
attach as shown using glue dots; trim ends.
Adhere smaller layers over ribbon using pop-
up glue dots.

FLEUR CARD
By Krista Halligan

Cardstock: olive green, metallic light pink
Printed floral paper by Anna Griffin
$1^1/2$" olive green ribbon, 18" long
Olive green StazOn ink pad (permanent ink)
Xyron with adhesive cartridge
Word stamp
Glue dots

Directions: Cut green card to $4^1/4$" x $5^1/4$".
Cut pink layer to 4" x $5^1/4$". Cut background
paper to $3^3/4$" x 5". Run ribbon through
Xyron machine. Stamp words using olive
green ink pad. Attach background paper to
pink layer. Fold ribbon in half and cut tails to
fit just under ribbon band. Attach with glue
dots. Attach ribbon band just over the top of
the ribbon tails. Adhere pink assembled layer
to card.

Cut-Outs

With the proliferation of punches available today, cut and punched shapes no longer have to remain one-dimensional. These snowflakes or flowers look as though they came right from nature with simple punched and shaped paper elements.

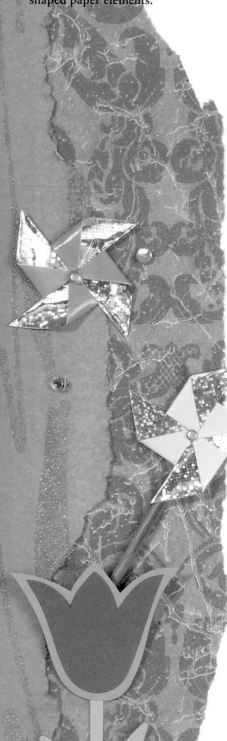

REINDEER POCKET CARD
By Sue Astroth

Cardstock: green, red, light & medium green textured
Philadelphia lower case "r" stencil by Making Memories
Maruyama mesh
Acrylic paints: metallic gold, dark green to match cardstock
Gold reindeer charm and jump ring
Gold safety pin
Reindeer die-cut by Meri Meri
Various alphabet stamps
"Happy" and "holidays" word stamps
3/8" red & green taffeta ribbon, 24" long
1/4" red satin ribbon, 6" long
Sewing machine and green thread
Krylon gold pen
Green dye ink pad
1/2" & 1" circle punches

Directions: Carefully pop out the "r" in the letter stencil and paint it gold. Paint the stencil background green. Set aside to dry. Cut one piece 4" x 2" from maruyama mesh. Paint with gold paint Make pocket same as Girley Girl card on page 24, using medium green textured cardstock. Cut one 4⁷/₈" x 4¹/₂" piece of red cardstock. Wrap red and green ribbon twice around red cardstock and tie a knot on front. Glue the red cardstock to top of pocket card just inside the stitching lines. Attach reindeer charm to safety pin with jump ring. Pin safety pin to knot on ribbon. Stamp "eindeer" on 2¹/₂" x ³/₄" piece of light green cardstock using green ink. Tear short edge. Place "r" into stencil background. With a dry brush, add a little gold paint to the background. Place maruyama mesh on upper left corner of red cardstock. Following photo, place "r" stencil, "eindeer" and reindeer die-cut on front of pocket; glue in place. Cut one piece 5¹/₂" x 4¹/₄" light green cardstock for tag and one piece 2" x 3¹/₂" red cardstock for accent. Stamp "happy" and "holiday" onto scraps of light green cardstock. Trim and edge with gold pen. Following photo, adhere to tag. Make reinforcement from red cardstock using punches. Punch a ¹/₂" circle at the top of the light green tag. Glue red reinforcement around the hole. Tie the satin ribbon to the tag with a slipknot.

SNOW POCKET CARD
By Sue Astroth

Cardstock: silver, blue, off-white
5/8" white ribbon, 1 yard
Philadelphia lower case "s" stencil by Making Memories
Acrylic paint: silver and blue to match cardstock
White die-cut snowflake
Blue safety pin
1" metal-rimmed tag
White snowflake button
"N-O-W" letters from vintage game cards
Krylon silver pen
Snowman stamp
Blue thread and sewing machine
1/2", 1", 1¹/₄" circle punches
Button shank cutter
Needle

Directions: Pop out the "s" in the letter stencil and paint silver. Paint in the stencil background blue. Make pocket the same as Girley Girl card on page 24 except use blue cardstock. Cut one 4⁷/₈" x 4¹/₂" piece of silver cardstock. Wrap ribbon twice around silver cardstock and tie a knot on the front. Punch out blue circle to cover metal-rimmed tag. Remove string from tag and set aside. Cut shank from snowflake button. Glue blue circle and button to tag. Using a needle, punch hole at top of tag. Tie string from tag through the tag hole and the end of the safety pin. Pin safety pin through ribbon knot. Glue the silver cardstock to top of pocket card, just inside stitching lines. Place "s" back into stencil background. With a dry brush add a little silver paint to the background as a highlight. Punch out "N-O-W" letters from game cards. Glue stencil, letters and snowflake in place. For tag cut 4¹/₄" x 5¹/₂" piece of silver cardstock, 2¹/₂" x 3³/₄" piece of blue cardstock and 2¹/₂" x 2¹/₄" piece of off-white cardstock. Stamp snowman on off-white cardstock and edge with silver pen; glue all layers in place. Punch hole at top of tag. Thread remaining ribbon through hole and tie in slipknot.

GILDED DRAGONFLY
By Krista Halligan

Cardstock: Metallic green, metallic copper
Patterned patina paper
Acetate
Permanent black ink pad
Xyron with adhesive cartridge
Metallic leafing
$^3/_8$" copper ribbon
$^1/_8$" hole punch
Dragonfly stamp by Heartfelt Impressions
Pop-Up Glue Dots

Directions: Make $4^1/_4$" x $5^1/_2$" folded card from green cardstock. Cut copper layer to 4" x $5^1/_4$". Cut patina paper layer to $3^3/_4$" x 5". Adhere all layers. Stamp dragonfly image on acetate using black permanent ink pad. Cut out image. Run through Xyron machine to apply adhesive to back of image. Cover adhesive with metallic leafing. Place dragonfly image on card layers using pop-up glue dots. Punch two holes at the top of card and thread with ribbon.

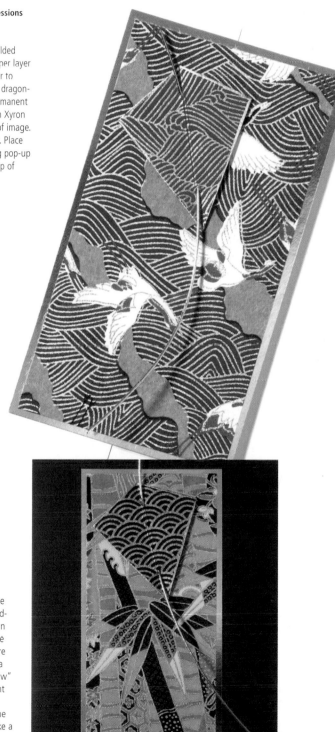

KITE CARDS
By Patty Carlson

Gold cardstock
Japanese washi paper, 2 coordinating
   patterns
Gold leafing pen
5" piece of gold mizuhiki paper cord
Emagination punch, kite shape
White or black card (tri-fold)
Xyron machine with adhesive cartridge
$^1/_8$" hole punch
Stylus
Sticky dots

Directions: Run pieces of washi paper through the Xyron machine. Cut one piece to $2^1/_2$" x 5" and adhere to the gold cardstock, which has been cut $^1/_4$" larger than the washi paper, leaving a gold edge. Take the other piece of washi paper and adhere to a scrap piece of cardstock. Punch out a kite shape. With a stylus and a ruler, "draw" a crease lengthwise on the kite from point to point. Fold on crease and punch two holes in the kite $^3/_8$" from each end of the crease. Insert the mizuhiki cord to look like a kite "tail." Edge kite with gold leafing pen. Glue the gold-edged card to left flap of folded card. On the back of the kite, place two sticky dots near the top. Turnover and adhere to front of card at an angle.

DAISY CARD
By Diana Diaz

Cardstock: natural, moss green
5¹/₂" square brown card
Daisy stamp by Make An Impression
Thank you stamp
Stylus
Radiant Pearls: yellow, brown, and greens
Black embossing ink pad
Clear embossing powder
Small petal & tiny flower punches
Gold foil and 2-way glue pen

Directions: Emboss 4" square frame with stylus on brown card. Stamp flowers on 3¹/₂" x 4" natural cardstock using black embossing pad. Emboss with clear embossing powder. Punch petals from natural paper. Paint with yellow and brown Radiant Pearls. Adhere image to 4¹/₄" x 3³/₄" moss green card, then to base card. Color image with Radiant Pearls as desired. Punch tiny flowers from gold and brown cardstock. Cover "frame" around flowers with 2-way glue. Set aside until tacky, then apply foil, colored side up. Adhere yellow petals as shown and tiny flower centers. Add small amount of gold glitter to center of punched flowers. Add thank you stamp.

GERANIUM CARD
By Diana Diaz

Natural-colored cardstock
Geranium stamp by Make An Impression
Black embossing pad
Clear embossing powder
Radiant Pearls, light & dark green and pink
³/₈" double-sided tape
3-flower corner punch
5¹/₂" square mauve paper
Blue Liquid Pearls
5" square blue metallic paper
Light blue ultra-fine glitter
Stylus

Directions: Stamp flower on natural cardstock with black embossing pad. Emboss with clear powder. Cut around outside of image as shown. Adhere to center of blue paper making sure to apply adhesive only in the middle. Color with Radiant Pearls. Adhere double-sided tape to form a frame around geranium; position tape under the extending leaves. Remove protective tape liner. Dust with glitter. Using a stylus and ruler, "draw" a line framing outside of the glitter tape. Adhere blue paper to 5¹/₄" square mauve card. Using a stylus, "draw" a line around the blue paper. Using mauve paper, punch flower petals and adhere with craft glue as shown. With a toothpick, add small dot of blue Liquid Pearls in center of each flower.

LEAVES
By Susan Gin

Cardstock: dark green, white
Mulberry paper with green leaves
Leaf stamps
Black permanent ink pad
Vellum: clear, light green, light peach
Water-based markers in yellows, greens, and oranges
Fine mist spray bottle of water
Double-sided tape

Directions: Layer white, dark green, and white cardstock on dark green card as shown. Adhere a torn sheet of mulberry paper on top. Stamp leaves on vellums using black ink pad. Color the front or back of leaves with markers using shades of yellows, greens, and oranges. Spray leaves with a fine mist of water and blot immediately with a tissue. Heat to dry completely. Paper may curl if heat is too hot. Cut out leaves and adhere to front of card with double-sided tape.

FLOWER FRAME TRI-FOLD
By Phyllis Nelson

Cardstock: light blue, white, violet
Flower frame stamp by Magenta
Stamps: small flower, border, sentiment
White pigment pad & white embossing powder
Twinkling H2O's paint in shades of violet, blue, & green
Lavender ink pad
$7/8$" violet sheer ribbon
$1/4$" white sheer ribbon

Directions: Emboss the flower frame twice on light blue cardstock using white ink and white embossing powder. On one image, paint the outside frame and inner flower image with Twinkling H2O's. On the second image, paint the inner square and circle. With the light blue cardstock, make two cards measuring 5" x 7". Overlap and glue these cards together so that one side opens on the right and the other side opens on the left. Trim around largest painted square frame and cut out center circle. Keep the center circle intact for later use. Cut two layering mats for largest frame in white and violet as shown. Glue these layers together. Using the square frame as a template, trace the square window opening and cut through both layers of the mats with a craft knife. Layer and glue embossed frame on the top. Glue unit on the card. Cut inside frame of card. On inside flap of card, stamp small flower image randomly using lavender ink. Set aside. With the second embossed image, cut inside square and, with a craft knife, remove center circle. Glue this square piece on inside of card so that it is framed by the outside opening. With craft knife, cut inner circle revealing the inside of the card. Stamp a border on a scrap of light blue using lavender ink. Trim and position just under the embossed square. Attach remaining center medallion to a square violet mat. Position on the inside of card so flower shows through circular window. Stamp greeting in lavender ink. Finish with violet and white ribbons on the side.

MEDALLION CARD
By Sandi Marr

Black cardstock, $8^1/2$" x $5^1/2$", folded in half
Medallion stamp by JudiKins
Clear embossing pad
Embossing powder in black, copper, gold
Double-sided tape

Directions: On the black card, emboss image with black embossing powder several times randomly. On a scrap of black paper, emboss the image twice in copper and once in gold. Cut out images and cut out the center. Cut through each circle at any point and intertwine the images alternating copper, gold, and copper. Attach to card in a vertical row using double-sided tape.

3-D Layers

Dimensional designs are featured here with layering and folded-paper techniques. Like a delicious cake, the more layers the better. Highlight an image, add a new accent color, or frame an image for dimension and change the basic design from simple to WOW!

GEOMETRIC DIMENSIONAL CARD
By Barbara Osada

Cardstock: tan, purple, turquoise, blue, black
Metallic green paper
Stamp by Paula Best
Scrap of mat board
Silver embossing powder and embossing pad
Pearl-Ex powders
Paper crimper, wave pattern
Raffia ribbon, rayon threads

Directions: Crimp the purple cardstock and attach to a tan card. Layer two rectangles of metallic green paper and the frayed raffia ribbon as shown. Layer the mat board scrap with a rectangle of turquoise cardstock on top. Emboss the geometric image with silver embossing powder on a piece of black cardstock. Color with Pearl-Ex powders and edge with blue cardstock. Tape the rayon threads to the back and attach to the mat board piece.

SQUARES & LAYERS
By Kathy Yee

Cardstock: blue, rust, gold
4-square floral stamp by Magenta
Gold pigment ink pad
Black dye-based ink pad
Gold embossing powder
Deckle-edge scissors
Foam mounting tape

Directions: Cut blue cardstock to 4³/4" x 9¹/2". Fold in half. Mount gold cardstock to the blue card leaving ¹/4" border. Stamp 4-square image once each on blue and rust cardstock embossing with gold pigment ink and gold embossing powder. Trim the blue and rust images close to the outside of the embossed line. With the large blue square, cut out 2 small squares from opposite diagonal corners and save. Cut close to embossed line and leave the blue inside border attached to the 2 remaining squares. This will be used to space the rust squares. Glue the connected blue squares on the gold cardstock. Cut out all 4 squares of the rust embossed image, close to the embossed lines. Referring to photo, replace the cut out blue squares with the rust squares on the gold cardstock. Glue in place. Take the 4 loose squares (2 of each color) and place them over the same image of the opposite color already glued to the gold cardstock. Make sure the images are oriented in the same direction. Cut the loose squares diagonally with the deckle-edge scissors. Consult the image as a cutting guide. Place the diagonally cut squares back over the identical image. Discard half of each square so that the blue half is on the outside and the rust is on the inside. Mount remaining half squares with foam mounting tape.

TWO HANDS AT SEA
By Barbara Osada

Cardstock: neutral, aqua, brown, rust
Decorative black and silver papers
Hand stamp by Above the Mark
Text stamp by Limited Edition
Postage stamp by Hero Art
Plume stamp by Stampendous
Black dye-based ink pad
Brown, taupe ink pads
Gold embossing powder and embossing pad
Scraps of patterned paper
Paper butterfly charm
Decorative scissors

Directions: On the aqua cardstock, emboss the plume image with embossing ink and gold embossing powder. Use the direct-to-paper technique to add the taupe ink. Stamp the hand image with black ink on the brown cardstock. Color the edges with the brown ink pad. Adhere squares of black and silver cardstock, the band with the sentiment at the top and the embossed rust band. Stamp the postal image on a scrap of cardstock and color with earth tones. Trim with decorative scissors. Finish with a gold paper butterfly charm.

EIFFEL TOWER CARD
By Krista Halligan

Cardstock: metallic silver, white glossy
Patterned Paper by 7gypsies
Embossed silver vellum by K & Company
³/8" white ribbon
¹/4" black trim
Black pigment ink & black embossing powder
Eiffel Tower stamp by Paper Parachute
Pop-Up glue dots
Directions: Cut silver cardstock to 4¹/4" x 5¹/2" when folded in half. Cut printed background to 4" x 5¹/4". Cut vellum to 3³/4" x 5". Stamp Eiffel Tower on white glossy cardstock using black pigment ink and emboss with black embossing powder. Assemble layers of the card as shown. Attach ribbon using glue dots. Attach Eiffel Tower to card over ribbon, using glue dots.

It is
Christmas
In the
Heart
That puts
Christmas
In the
Air

W.T. Ellis

TRANSPARENCY TREE
By Debby DeBenedetti

Cardstock: light green, medium green
Transparency film
**5-6 paper scraps with various textures,
    approx.. 2" wide, cut into assorted shapes**
Holiday motif stamp (vertical orientation)
Dye-based ink pad
Brad
1/8" hole punch

Directions: Cut medium green paper 4" x 9" and light green paper 3³/4" x 8³/4". Cut monogram letter out of scrap paper and place on a small mat. Using the computer, print holiday message on transparency film. Message should be vertically oriented. Stamp holiday image on the smaller sheet of paper, lining up with text on transparency film. Layer 2 sheets of paper with smaller one on top and adhere. Lay transparency on top. Punch hole, centered approximately 1/2" from top edge. Arrange scraps on top of each other as shown and punch hole. Punch hole in monogram; place on top of scraps. Place monogram stack on top of transparency and align holes. Insert brad through all layers and secure in back. NOTE: Small holiday die-cuts could be substituted for scraps.

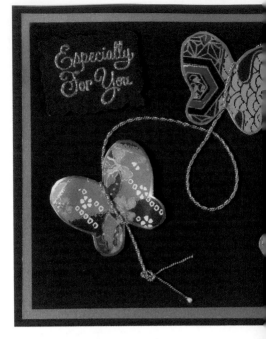

WOMAN IN PINK
By Sandi Marr

Black cardstock, 5" x 4¹/2"
Woman stamp by Paper Parachute
4 pink brads
Pink glossy paper, 5¹/2 " x 9¹/2" folded
**Pink decorative paper with gold flecks
    4³/4" x 4¹/4"**
**Black plastic stitchery grid, 3¹/2" x 4¹/8"
    (available at craft stores)**
Scrap of pink glossy paper
Black StazOn ink pad
Double-sided tape
Foam mounting tape

Directions: Stamp image on scrap of pink glossy paper using the black StazOn ink pad and cut out. Attach the plastic grid to the decorative pink paper using a brad in each corner. Layer on the black cardstock using double-sided tape. This will conceal the backs of the brads. Use double-sided tape to layer all three pieces to the folded glossy pink card. Attach the stamped image to the plastic grid using foam mounting tape.

A GIFT FOR YOU
By Kathy Yee

Cardstock: olive green, white
Tiny word stamps
Bag template by Hanko Designs
Washi and coordinating tissue paper
Red pigment ink pad
Mizuhiki cord
Gold thread
1/8" hole punch
Foam mounting tape

Directions: Using the purse template, draw, cut and fold the bag from white cardstock. Tape the back of the purse to secure. Use the template to cut a piece of washi paper to cover the front of the bag and adhere. Stuff the bag with matching tissue paper. Attach a small piece of Mizuhiki cord to form a handle and tape to the inside of the purse. Make a small tag using a scrap piece of matching cardstock and stamp "For You" with red pigment ink. Punch 1/8" hole and attach to the bag handle using gold string. Adhere the bag to the green card using foam mounting tape.

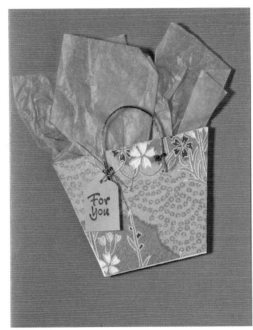

ASIAN BUTTERFLIES
By Kathy Yee

Cardstock: red, gold
Butterfly stickers by Hanko Design
Message stamp by Stamp Francisco
Metallic gold ink pad
Egyptian Gold embossing powder by JudiKins
Gold cord, 20" long
Foam mounting tape

Directions: Make base card from red cardstock. Adhere gold then red cardstock to the folded 4¹/₄" x 5¹/₂" red card. Adhere three butterfly stickers to gold cardstock and trim leaving a small border of gold around the butterflies. Starting with the butterfly to be mounted in the left bottom corner, knot one end of the gold cord then wrap around a butterfly. Tape the cord in place on the back side of the butterfly. Use foam mounting tape to attach the first butterfly to the red cardstock. Form a loop with the gold cord and then repeat wrapping and attaching the next two butterflies. Emboss words with gold ink and Egyptian Gold embossing powder on red cardstock and adhere with foam mounting tape.

PINWHEEL CARD
By Kathy Yee

Cardstock: white, light green, plum
Botanical background paper
Pinwheel stamps by Magenta
Various small image stamps
Gold pigment and metallic ink pads
Gold embossing powder
Foam mounting tape

Directions: Using the white cardstock, cut and fold a 5¹/₂" square base card. Stamp various small stamps randomly on the plum cardstock with metallic gold ink. Adhere to the folded white card, followed by the light green cardstock. Next, adhere the botanical paper to the light green cardstock. Stamp 2 each of the "pinwheels" on white, light green and plum cardstock with gold pigment ink. Emboss using gold embossing powder. Cut out stamped images leaving a small border around the embossed edges. Stamp the center image on plum cardstock, embossing with gold pigment ink and gold embossing powder. Cut image close to embossed edges. Mount the pinwheels with foam mounting tape on the outside edge and glue at the center, alternating colors. Mount the center with foam mounting tape.

3-D GRAPES
By Beckie Torgerson

Cardstock: cream, burgundy, dark green, light green, dark purple, light purple, pearl gloss in white or cream
Grapes stamp by Holly Berry House Originals
Script stamp by A Stamp in the Hand
Black pigment ink
Black Brilliance Ink
Gold embossing powder
Clear or Prisms Ultra Fine Glitter
Dye-based ink pads: butterscotch, eggplant, meadow, cranberry
Leafing adhesive
Gold leaf
Southwest Corner Punch by Marvy
Gold string
Stipple brushes
Foam mounting tape

Directions: Fold cream cardstock to make 5" x 6¹/₂" card. Cut burgundy cardstock to 4 ⁵/₈" x 6¹/₈". Punch corners. Cut white glossy cardstock to 3⁷/₈" x 5¹/₂" and stamp grapes with black Brilliance Ink. Apply dye-based inks with stipple brush. Stamp words randomly on cardstock. Apply ink to stamp and stamp once lightly on scrap paper, then stamp on glossy stock. Do not re-ink stamp but stamp again to let words fade. Stamp and emboss grapes once on green cardstock. Stamp and emboss grapes twice on both shades of purple cardstock. Cut out entire image from light green cardstock. Mount on cream cardstock over stamped image. Layer image of grapes using foam tape. Cut upper leaf only from dark green cardstock. Mount to light green image. Cut full grape bunch from dark purple paper; mount to light green image. Cut grape bunch from light purple cardstock removing some of the grapes so that when layered, some of the dark purple grapes are visible from the layer below. Do the same with the next dark purple and light purple images. Using a glue pen, highlight bottom edges of grapes and sprinkle with glitter. Apply leafing adhesive randomly to grape leaves. Apply gold leaf. Wrap burgundy cardstock with gold string and mount to folded card. Attach grape image to burgundy cardstock.

Tearing

Tearing is a simple way to mimic the deckle edge of expensive paper and visually extends the image past the torn edge. Tear shapes freehand or use a deckle ruler to give a soft antiqued or vintage look.

HARLEQUIN QUEEN
By Krista Halligan

Cardstock: white parchment
Patterned paper by 7gypsies
Black with white dots ribbon
Ranger Distress Ink pads: Antique Linen, Old Paper, Vintage Photo, Walnut Stain, Black Soot
Stamps by Invoke Arts, Creative Block
Gold crown embellishment

Directions: Fold 8$^1/2$" x 11" parchment sheet in half to make 8$^1/2$" x 5$^1/2$" card. Cut patterned paper to 8$^1/4$" x 5$^1/4$". Cut 2 white parchment pieces to 8$^1/2$" x 5$^1/2$". Distress one white parchment piece using the Ranger Distress Inks. Start with the lightest colors first (Antique Linen and Old Paper), and apply pad directly to paper, rubbing color on in a circular motion. Crumple paper, then smooth out. Proceed with distressing using Vintage Photo & Tea Dye pads until the desired effect is achieved. Add some Walnut Stain & Black Soot. Stamp word background in Vintage Photo. Tear edges of paper to approximately 4$^1/2$" x 5 $^1/2$". Darken edges with Walnut Stain & Black Soot Distress pads. Distress second piece of white parchment, but do not crumple. Stamp lady image in black. Cut layer to approximately 5$^1/4$" x 3". Darken edges. Assemble layers of the card, placing ribbon under the word background as shown. Attach gold crown.

GRAPES TAG
By Sue Astroth

Cardstock: cream linen, dark green
Patterned paper
4 gold eyelets
Dye-based ink: purple, ochre, green
Purple pigment ink
Clear and gold embossing powders
Black pen
Script background stamp by A Stamp in the Hand
Grapes stamp
Label stamp
Foam mounting tape
7/8" sheer violet ribbon, 12" long
Eyelet and setting tools
1/2" circle punch
Stipple brushes

Directions: Create grape paper on cream cardstock by stamping script and grapes randomly using both green and purple ink. Cut out tag. Tear strip of decorative paper to fit along left side of tag. For a vintage look, stipple tag with purple and ochre dye-based ink. Stamp grapes on cream cardstock with purple pigment ink. Emboss with clear embossing powder. Tear out image to measure approximately 3" x 4¹/2". Add more color to grapes with stipple brushes. Set one eyelet in each corner. Adhere to tag at angle with foam tape. Stamp label on cream cardstock and emboss in gold. Cut close to image. Write message in label and adhere to tag. Mat the entire tag with dark green cardstock leaving just ¹/16" of the green showing. Punch circle at top of tag, thread with ribbon and tie bow.

TROPICAL CARD
By Connie Baldonado

Cardstock: mustard, kraft, sage green, white
Colored Hawaiian image
Hawaiian themed stamps for background and embellishment
Pigment ink pads: Sea Glass, gold, black by Clearsnap
Black detail embossing powder
Tan string, 3 yards long
Sea shell (with hole for stringing)
Sage green marker

Directions: Stamp 11" x 5¹/2" piece of mustard and 5" x 4¹/2" piece of kraft cardstock with background stamp, using Sea Glass ink pad. Fold mustard cardstock in half to make a 5¹/2" square card. Round corners. Stamp background stamp on 6" x 7" piece of sage cardstock with gold ink; let dry. Tear to desired size (approx.. 4" x 5¹/2"). Tear tropical image on all edges so that it's slightly smaller than sage layer. Stamp greeting stamp on white cardstock and emboss with black embossing powder. For a vintage look, highlight image with sage marker. Adhere layers as shown. Wrap string around card at fold. Tie with loop. Thread string through hole in shell and knot.

HELLO
By Jenn Gaub

Cardstock: cream, lime
Patterned paper
Sandpaper
Embroidery floss and sewing needle
Dimensional flowers
Beads, pearls (flower centers)
"Hello" stamp by Hero Arts
Green dye-based ink pad

Directions: Distress the edges of four 2¹/2" squares of patterned paper using sandpaper. Make holes with a sewing needle in the corner of each square and stitch a frame using a matching color of embroidery floss. Make a 5³/4" square base card from cream cardstock. Attach a 5¹/2" square of lime to the base card. Glue the colored squares in place; adhere dimensional flowers with beads for flower centers. Using green ink pad, stamp word on lime paper and adhere as shown.

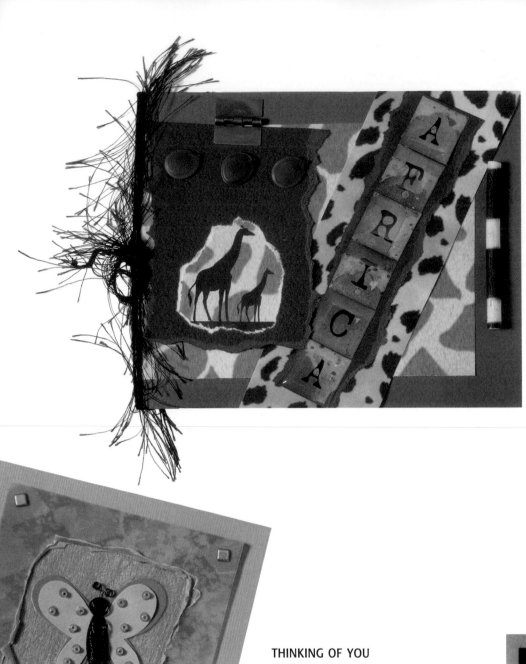

AFRICA CARD
By Sandi Allan

Cardstock: brown, dark brown
Assorted African and animal print paper
Alphabet tiles
Metal hinge
Animal/ African embellishments
Seeds
Black eyelash fiber

Directions: Cut brown cardstock to 5" x 12". Cut animal print paper to 4" x 10½". Center animal print and glue to brown cardstock. Fold in half. Cut a 2" strip from a contrasting animal print paper. Glue diagonally from the top right corner of card. Trim excess paper at top and bottom of card. Cut a 2" x 5" strip of dark brown cardstock. Adhere alphabet tiles in the center of the strip to spell the word, "AFRICA". Carefully tear side edges. Glue to diagonal strip. Cut a 3" x 3¾" strip of dark brown cardstock. Glue one end of hinge to top of strip. Let dry. Tear all edges except top. Tear a small image from African paper and glue to front of strip. Glue top end of hinge to top of card. Glue African embellishment on right side of card. Glue three seeds to top of hinged strip. Inside card glue a 2" x 7" strip of African print onto bottom half of right side of card. It should overlap on the right edge of card by an inch. Fold excess over onto back of card; adhere. Finish card by wrapping at the fold with black eyelash fiber. Knot in the front. Trim excess.

THINKING OF YOU
By Jenn Gaub

Periwinkle cardstock piece
Periwinkle base card
Square brads
Patterned vellum
Periwinkle decorative paper
Paper Bliss 3-D butterfly
Greeting stamp
Black ink pad

Directions: Tear out center of 3½" square of vellum to make approximately 2" square hole. Repeat with a matching size of periwinkle cardstock. Stack the pieces together and roll the torn edges outward. Position and adhere a 2½" piece of decorative paper to the base card so that it will be seen when the torn window is in place. Add the butterfly embellishment. Secure the window piece with four square brads. Stamp greeting at bottom of card.

VINTAGE HEART
By Krista Halligan

Cardstock: white parchment, black
Patterned paper
Black & white ribbon
Ranger Distress Ink pads: Antique Linen, Old
    Paper, Vintage Photo, Tea Dye, Walnut
    Stain, Black Soot
Heart stamp by Stampington & Co.
Glue Dots and Pop-Up Glue Dots

Directions: Cut black cardstock to 6" x 6"
when folded. Cut white parchment to 6" x
6" or larger. Cut printed paper to 4³/₄" x
4³/₄". Cut 2 pieces white parchment to 4¹/₄"
x 5¹/₂". Distress all white parchment pieces
using the Distress Ink pads. Start with lightest
colors first (Antique Linen and Old Paper).
Apply pad directly to paper, rubbing on color
in a circular motion. Crumple paper and
smooth out. Proceed with distressing using
Vintage Photo and Tea Dye pads until the
desired effect is achieved. Add Walnut Stain
and Black Soot for a darker look. Tear edges
of paper to approximately 5³/₄" x 5³/₄".
Darken edges with Walnut Stain and Black
Soot. Assemble and adhere card layers.
Attach ribbon as shown, using glue dots.
Stamp heart image and cut out. Attach heart
to card over ribbon, using pop-up glue dots.

PRIZED BIRD DOG
By Terrece Siddoway

Cardstock: tan, cream, navy
Black dye-based ink pad
Water-based markers
Dog Stamp by Personal Stamp Exchange
Geese stamp

Directions: Fold 8¹/₂" x 5¹/₂" tan cardstock in half to make base card. Cut a piece
of navy blue cardstock 5" x 3³/₄" and
adhere to card. Stamp geese on cream cardstock with black ink pad. Cut to 4³/₄" x
3¹/₂" and glue to blue mat. Stamp dog on
cream cardstock. Color with markers as
shown. Tear away excess cream cardstock
approximately ¹/₄" from image outline.
Adhere to a piece of navy blue cardstock
and cut approximately ¹/₄" from image outline. Attach to card in lower right corner.

ROMAN CORNICE
By Barbara Osada

Cardstock: olive brown, black, tan, gray
Natural-colored handmade paper
Roman numerals by Above the Mark
Roman Column by A Stamp in the Hand
1/4" metallic ribbon, 5" long
Ink pads: black, taupe, brown, olive
Gold embossing powder and embossing pad
Roman cornice stamps
Miscellaneous collage stamps
Corner punch
Foam dots

Directions: Fold olive brown cardstock in
half to make 5¹/₂" x 8" base card. Layer the
black cardstock and handmade natural
paper as shown. On the tan cardstock,
stamp the large column image with black
ink. Add script and numerals to side and
bottom. Using the direct-to-paper technique,
apply the olive ink to give an aged look.
Attach gold ribbon as shown. Emboss the
small cornice image on gray cardstock, using
gold embossing powder. Detail the edges
using the corner punch. Stamp with the floral stamp in taupe ink and edge with a
brown ink pad. Attach to the card with foam
dots.

Beads

Think of beautiful beads as jewelry for cards. Beads come in all shapes, sizes, and materials. They offer a great way to add texture and a bit of pizazz. Whether using one large bead, a variety of small ones, or covering shapes with microbeads, you'll find they add elegance and sparkle to your cards.

SEA LIFE
By Linda Lavasani

Cardstock: medium green, dark green, white
Stamps: Fish and Coral by Fred Mullet, Spiral by Hero Arts, miscellaneous ocean life
Colorbox Cat's Eye Chalk Ink pads: Robin's Egg, Sky Blue, French Blue, Warm Green, Lime Green, Amber Clay, Creamy Brown
Red & black dye ink pads
Colorbox Mica Magic green ink pad
Small piece of mica
2 brads, 2 small spacer beads
Small snail shell
Fibers, broken shell bits, charms, beads

Directions: Cut medium green, dark green and white cardstock into tags as shown. Make a mask of both the fish and the seahorse images. NOTE: You will need both pieces of the masks so cut them out carefully. On the white cardstock use Amber Clay and Creamy Brown ink pads to color in the sea floor. Stamp the seahorse in black ink. Using the outside mask, color in with Amber Clay ink. Stamp the coral image in the lower right corner using Warm Green ink. Using the direct-to-paper technique, ink in the remaining background with Robin's Egg, Sky Blue and Lime Green to create the look of water. Stamp the fish image in red ink. Mask the outside of the fish and use a little more lime green ink to brighten the image, then highlight the outer edge of the fish. Mask the fish and stamp three seaweed stalks using Warm Green ink. Randomly stamp spirals in French Blue ink in the water area. Stamp a seaweed image on the piece of mica, using the green Mica Magic ink. Let dry. Put two small holes in the mica and attach it to the tag using the brads and spacer beads. (The spacer beads go under the mica.) Attach the snail shell using clear adhesive. Layer the piece on the medium green cardstock and then the light green cardstock. Embellish with fibers, beads, and shells.

WINE CHARMS GIFT CARD
By Terrece Siddoway

Cardstock: purple, olive green
Dye-based markers: deep purple, plum,
    olive green
Charms
Beads
Wire rings
Craft knife and cutting mat
Stamps by Art Impressions: bottle, goblet,
    grape cluster
Double-sided tape

Directions: Cut 8$^{1}/_{2}$" x 5$^{1}/_{2}$" purple cardstock and fold in half for base card. Cut
olive green cardstock to 3$^{3}/_{4}$" x 5". Color
directly on stamps with markers. Stamp on
olive paper as shown. Using a craft knife,
cut slits on each side of the bottle neck and
glass stem. Make wine charms by stringing
two beads, one charm, and two more beads
on each wire ring. Attach three rings
through slits for each image. Attach olive
layer to card with a liberal application of
double-sided tape to cover all areas.

AUTUMN HARVEST MINI BOOK
By Iraci Bautista

Cardstock: rust
Text weight paper
Leaf stamp
Strip of handmade textured paper
Gold metallic ink pad
Painted fabric piece
Eyelets
Tag
Paper piercer
Silk leaf in fall colors
Fibers
Beads
Gold wire

Directions: Stamp leaves onto one side of
8$^{1}/_{2}$" x 6" rust cardstock, using gold metallic
ink pad. Fold the cardstock in half; also fold
four 8$^{1}/_{2}$" x 6" sheets of text weight paper
in half to create a book. The cardstock will
serve as the cover and the text weight paper
will be the pages. Pierce three evenly spaced
holes in the center of the spine through all
pages and cover. Weave wire through end
holes from outside to inside of spine and out
through the middle hole. Place a bead on
wire and wrap around wire. Continue to add
a bead and wrap wire until spine is full of
beads. Bend tails into spirals. Create a book
wrap with a strip of handmade paper. Punch
a hole on each end of strip, adhere painted
fabric piece, and set eyelets. The eyelets hold
the pieces together. String fibers through eyelets and add a hand painted circle tag.
Adhere silk leaf.

GLASS BEAD KOI FISH
By Barbara Osada

Cardstock: black, turquoise, white, gold
Koi fish stamp by JudiKins
Asian block stamp
Black pigment ink pad
Black & copper embossing powders and
**   embossing pads**
Clear microbeads
Double-sided adhesive sheet
Colored markers

Directions: Cut the turquoise cardstock and glue to the 4^1/$_4$" x 5^1/$_2$" black folded card as shown. On white cardstock, emboss the koi fish image with a black pigment ink pad and black embossing powder. Color the image with markers. Cut a piece of double-sided adhesive and apply the microbeads beads over the image. Press gently to set the beads. Trim, leaving a narrow edge of white. On a small square of gold cardstock, emboss the Asian block image with clear embossing ink and copper embossing powder. Trim and attach to the corner of the card.

ASIAN TRI-FOLD
By Kathy Yee

Cardstock: red, black
Washi paper
Small flower stamp by Magenta
Metallic gold ink pad
Krylon gold pen
24-gauge copper wire
Sea glass
Two beads
Bamboo skewer
Double-sided tape
Foam mounting tape

Directions: Cut red cardstock to 8^1/$_2$" x 5^1/$_2$". Fold by scoring 2^1/$_8$" from each short end and fold toward the center to form a 3-panel card. Stamp small flowers randomly on the front two panels of the tri-folded card using metallic gold ink. Outline the front two panels using the gold pen. Set aside to dry. Mount 1^3/$_8$" x 4^3/$_4$" washi strips to two 1^5/$_8$" x 5" pieces of black cardstock. Use small pieces of foam mounting tape to attach the black cardstock to the front panels of the tri-fold card. Wrap copper wire 3–4 times around the piece of sea glass. Twist together at the bottom several times then string two beads on both strands of wire. Use the skewer to shape the wire into loops between the beads and add curls at the ends. Use a small piece of double-sided tape to attach the beaded sea glass to the left front panel.

BABY BEADS

By Susan Thompson

Cardstock: pink plaid, white with pink polka dots
2" circle punch
Hanger stamp by Dolphin Song
Dress stamp by Personal Stamp Exchange
White wire for beading
Alphabet beads
Pink filler beads
Pink brads
Green pigment ink pad
Clear embossing ink pad
Clear & silver embossing powders
Foam mounting tape

Directions: Punch circle in front of card. Stamp wire hanger on inside of card so that it is framed by the circle; emboss in silver. Stamp dress in green on white cardstock and emboss in clear. Cut out. Use foam mounting tape to adhere dress over hanger on inside of card. String alphabet beads on wire as shown. Secure loops at wire ends to the card using pink brads.

WATERLILIES

By Linda Lavasani

Cardstock: black, metallic blue
Water lily stamps by Stamp Zia
Radiant Pearls: Dandelion Green, Sea Weed, Fandango Green, Royal Gold, Morning Glory, Royal Satin, Cool Water
Ink pads: black pigment, metallic gold
Black embossing powder
Fibers, beads

Directions: Stamp the large water lily image on black cardstock and emboss with black embossing powder. Using Radiant Pearls, paint the lily pads with a combination of all the greens and the gold, the lilies with the purples, and the water with blue. Mask the image. With gold ink, stamp the small waterlily. Use a craft knife to cut out the upper portion of the image and layer the blue metallic cardstock behind. Trim to size and layer on black 6" square folded card. Embellish with fibers and beads.

Buttons

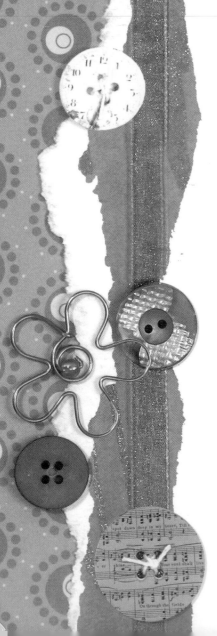

Button, button, everyone has buttons. They can be found clustered or as a single accent. The fun is hunting for vintage mother-of-pearl buttons or shopping for new shapes and styles. Attach them with a couple of quick stitches or a dab of glue and voilà!

CROWN TAG
By Sue Astroth

Light green cardstock
Scrap cream cardstock
Large brown kraft tag, 3 1/8" x 6"
19–25 vintage pearl buttons
Scrap from old book page
Crown charm
Two gold eyelets and setting tools
Gold wire
1/2" violet rayon ribbon, 10" long
Foam tape

Directions: Cut light green cardstock 3 1/2" x 6". Tear 1/2" from bottom of kraft tag. Tear book page into heart shape about 2 1/2" x 3". Glue in place on tag. Glue pearl buttons around edge. Using foam tape, glue crown charm inside heart. Cut cream cardstock to measure 2 1/2" x 1". Tear off 1/4" along each long edge. Adhere to tag below heart. Set gold eyelets. Wrap scrap of gold wire through eyelets and attach on back of tag. Glue entire tag on light green cardstock. Trim to 1/16" around tag. Using the kraft tag hole as a guide, punch a hole through the green cardstock. Thread with violet ribbon and tie into a bow.

THIS LITTLE PIGGY
By Terrece Siddoway

White cardstock
Pink & white dotted paper
Button Pig by Paper Bliss
Oval paper punch

Directions: Cut cardstock $5^1/2$" x $8^1/2$" and fold in half for base card. Trim pink paper to 4" x $5^1/2$" and glue to card. Punch oval from white cardstock. Glue just above center of card. Attach Button Pig. Inside sentiment: "Hope you're in the pink soon."

SISTERS
By Linda Lavasani

Cardstock: rust, burgundy & white print, tan
Sisters stamp by Stampington & Co.
Ink pads: rust, light brown, black ink
Embellishments: skeleton leaf, old key, vintage buttons & lace, fibers, beads
Diamond Glaze by JudiKins

Directions:
Distress the cardstock with the rust and brown inks. Stamp the image in black ink onto tan cardstock and distress with light brown ink and by sanding and tearing it. Tear a piece of the burgundy and white paper and lay it diagonally across the solid rust cardstock. Layer that onto the tan and then to the dotted piece. Adhere the stamped image to the card and edge two sides with lace using Diamond Glaze as the adhesive. Adhere the leaf and key above the stamped image. Glue the buttons to the ends of the lace and in the corner to help keep it securely in place. Further embellish with fibers and beads.

DAISIES
By Phyllis Nelson

Cardstock: bright pink, white
Lime green patterned paper
$3/8$" daisy print ribbon, 8" long
$1/4$" green plaid ribbon, 8" long
Three buttons
Stylus
Daisy brass embossing template

Directions: Using pink cardstock, fold 10" x 7" paper to make base card. Fold 5" x 7" green patterned paper in half to fit across top of card. Match folds and adhere. Glue two coordinating ribbons across the card as shown. Emboss daisy images three times on white paper. Cut out. Adhere daisies to pink border. Glue tiny buttons to the center of each daisy.

Sewing & Weaving

The sewing machine isn't just for fabric any more. Use basic stitches, colorful cardstock, and contrasting thread, to create pockets or decorative accents on your cards. Or try your hand at Papuela, an intricate paper-weaving technique that reinterprets woven fabric patterns.

TRAVEL COLLAGE
By Linda Lavasani

Cardstock: mustard, teal, burgundy, white
Black solvent-based ink
Colorbox Cat's Eye Chalk Ink pads: Sky Blue, Ice Blue, Yellow Citrus, Amber Clay, Tangerine, Lime Pastel, Rouge, Ice Jade, Aquamarine
Travel Collage Stamp
Southwest Corner punch by Marvy
Burgundy thread

Directions: Stamp the image onto white cardstock using black ink; heat set. Using the direct-to-paper technique, color in the image with the Cat's Eye ink pads. Cut out the image and layer on burgundy cardstock. Punch the corners of the teal cardstock and then attach to the burgundy piece. Randomly wrap the burgundy thread around the image using the corner detail as anchors; secure on the back with tape. Attach to the mustard card.

REINDEER TAG
By Sue Astroth

Cardstock: green, red
Green dye-based ink pad
Scrap light green cardstock
Reindeer die-cut by Meri Meri
Alphabet stamps
$1/2$" green rayon ribbon, 12" long
Sewing machine and green thread
$1/2$" circle punch

Directions: Cut two pieces of green cardstock with the following measurements: $3^1/4$" x 6" and $2^1/2$"x 3". Cut a piece of red cardstock $3^1/4$" x $5^3/4$". Center red cardstock on large sheet of green cardstock and sew in place, stitching $1/8$" from edge. Place remaining green cardstock rectangle on red cardstock $1/2$" from bottom and centered on both sides. Sew in place $1/8$" from edge. Glue reindeer die-cut on green rectangle. Stamp the word "reindeer" on small light green scrap of cardstock. Trim and glue to card. Punch hole at top of tag. Thread ribbon through hole and tie into bow.

CIRCLE PAPUELA
By Gail Martin

Cardstock: pink, burgundy
Gold paper (origami or cardstock)
Papuela Template PU0022 by Ecstasy Crafts
Papuela tools
Instruction book: *Papuela, the Basics of Paper Weaving by Nellie Snellen*
¹/₈" metallic ribbon
Corner punches (optional)
Embellishments: ribbon and paper flowers
Double-sided tape

Directions: Make a 5¹/₄" square base card from pink cardstock. Using removable tape, affix template with to the 4" square of pink cardstock. Follow papuela directions from instruction book. Decorating the completed project may include the use of corner stickers or corner punches. The circle opening may be lined with specialty paper. Mount the woven piece on a 4¹/₂" square of burgundy cardstock using double-sided tape then adhere to the 4³/₄" square of gold paper. Adhere to the folded card. Embellish with ribbon and flowers, charms, or vellum punched shapes.

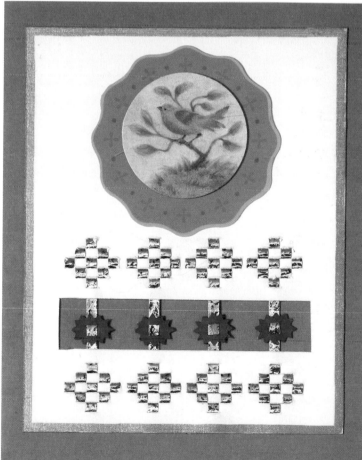

PAPUELA WITH RECTANGULAR OPENING
By Gail Martin

Blue cardstock
Papuela Template PU0009 by Ecstasy Crafts
Papuela tools
Instruction book: *Papuela, the Basics of Paper Weaving by Nellie Snellen*
¹/₈" gold metallic ribbon
Small heart, flower, or star punch
Double-sided tape

Directions: Make a 4¹/₄" x 5¹/₂" base card using blue cardstock. Cut a piece of blue cardstock to 3⁷/₈" x 5". Affix template with removable tape to cardstock. Follow directions in instruction book for basic papuela method. The ribbon is placed across the opening. Using double-sided tape on the back of the cardstock; tape over the ends of the ribbon and at the edges of the cardstock. Add a stamped piece or embellishment to the top half of the woven piece. Edge piece with metallic gold ink. Affix to the folded card, centering the woven piece.

WOVEN CARD
By Beckie Torgerson

Cardstock: dark blue, seven colors of choice
    for weaving
Text weight paper for backing
Various stamps for paper strip background
Script stamp by A Stamp in the Hand
Text stamp
Shrink plastic & heat tool
Fibers
Versamark ink pad by Tsukineko
Pearl-Ex powders
Graphite Black Brilliance ink
White Brilliance ink
Various pigment inks
Word stamp for tag

Directions: Make 4" x 9$^{1}/_{4}$" base card, using dark blue cardstock. Randomly stamp miscellaneous images on 4" x 11" strips of seven different cardstock colors, using black or white ink. Cut into $^{3}/_{8}$" x 11" strips. Apply adhesive to back of strips and apply to text weight paper alternating colors. Repeat colors until sheet is full or all of strips are used. (Makes enough for two cards.) Cut layered strips $^{3}/_{8}$" wide crosswise across strips to form small strips of squares. Stamp script stamp with Versamark ink pad on base card. Brush on assorted Pearl-Ex powders. Starting with center strip, apply to center of card toward the middle. Cut off part of the strip at the upper end to allow rows to build upward on each side (see photo). Place each column to the sides of the center layer, moving up one square to create colored points; cut off excess material at top. Stamp text on shrink plastic with Brilliance ink. Color using pigment inks. Shrink the plastic with a heat tool. Attach fibers and shrink plastic embellishment to the card.

MULTI-STENCIL BIRTHDAY CARD
By Gail Martin

Cardstock: rose, purple, dark sand
Erica Fortgens "December" Template
Instruction book: *New Ideas with*
    Embroidery on Paper by Erica Fortgens
Corner punches (optional)
Flower punch
Message stamp

Directions: Make a 5$^{1}/_{8}$" square base card, using rose cardstock. Using the pattern on page 78 of the instruction book, pierce the pattern on a 4$^{1}/_{2}$" square of dark sand cardstock. Follow directions from the book to cut and embroider. Punch corners of sand square and 4$^{3}/_{4}$" purple square, if desired. Assemble pieces. Punch a medium 6-petal flower from the scrap paper. Stamp message and glue to center of the card.

GOLDEN STAR
By Gail Martin

Black cardstock
Instruction book: *New Ideas with*
    Embroidery on Paper by Erica Fortgens
Gold origami paper or cardstock
Metallic gold embroidery thread and needle

Directions: Make a 5$^{1}/_{8}$" square base card, using black cardstock. Using the pattern on page 164 of the instruction book, pierce the pattern on a 4$^{1}/_{4}$" black cardstock square. Embroider using metallic gold thread, following the pattern in the book. Secure thread ends on the reverse of the card with small pieces of tape. Adhere embroidered piece to a 4$^{3}/_{4}$" square of gold paper then adhere to black card.

PLAY BOOK
By Sue Astroth

Cardstock: red, orange, yellow, blue, green purple (one 12" x 12" sheet of each)

Scraps of blue, orange, green, yellow cardstock for cover decoration

Three ¼" blue plastic split rings

"Play" sticker letters by Provo Craft

Black thread

⅜" circle punch

Sewing machine

Directions: Cut red, orange, yellow, blue, green and purple cardstock in 6" x 6" squares. To make a page, stack two 6" x 6" pieces of the same color. Sew all colored pairs together for a total of twelve pages. Determine the color sequence of the pages. Punch holes along one side of each of the pages 1¼" from both the top and bottom. Punch the third hole equidistant from the other two. Stack pages together and place split rings through the holes. Decorate cover page with cardstock scraps and "Play" stickers as shown.

Clay

These beautiful cards use clay as a dimensional focal point. Clay may be shaped by hand, formed with a mold, or rolled flat and impressed with rubber stamps. Once cured, it can be painted, embellished with Pearl-Ex, or adorned with gold leaf for endless options.

AFRICAN MASK
By Barbara Osada

Cardstock: blue, violet, turquoise, black, white
Metallic back-gold paper
Petroglyph stamp by Stamp Out Cute
Mask mold
Black polymer clay
Pearl-Ex powders
Ink pads: black, earth-toned
Fibers, dried twigs
Tacky glue

Directions: On a 4$\frac{1}{4}$" x 6$\frac{1}{4}$" blue folded card, layer the black/gold metallic, black, purple, and turquoise papers (see photo). Stamp the petroglyph image in black onto the white cardstock. Tear the edges, crumple tightly, and unfold. With the earth-toned ink pads, use the direct-to-paper technique to color the image. Ink torn edges with a turquoise ink pad and attach to the card. Make polymer clay mask using black clay and mold. Dust the mask with Pearl-Ex powders before baking. Secure the dried twigs, fibers, and mask with tacky glue.

POLYMER CLAY TILE CARDS
By Patty Carlson

Cardstock, decorative paper
Polymer clay in black and 3 other coordinating colors (such as magenta, purple, blue)
Leafing foil in variegated colors
Clay cutters in square shapes
Pasta machine
Toaster oven
Krylon gold pen
Polymer clay glaze
Sandpaper

Directions: Condition clay thoroughly. Roll a piece of the black clay in a shape approximately 4" square on the #2 setting of the pasta machine. Lay clay on work surface. Tear off small pieces of coordinating colors of clay and press them into the black clay dotting the entire surface randomly. Then press small pieces of the leafing foil on the clay surface, overlapping onto some of the colors. Carefully take the clay piece and run through the #2 setting of the pasta machine. Turn the piece (never fold clay) and run through the pasta machine on the #3 setting. Turn again and repeat. The foil should have a crackle effect. Lay piece out again on work surface. Cut with square cutter and put the tiles on cardboard. Bake tiles in oven according to clay package instructions. NOTE: Pasta machine and oven should not be used for food preparation. When cool, sand sides of the tiles to keep them square and smooth. Brush on glaze and let dry. Edge each tile with gold pen. Glue three tiles on decorative paper and adhere to card.

FLORENTINE "A" CARD
By Barbara Osada

Cardstock: white, tan, black, metallic black-gold
Collage stamp by Inkadinkado
Plume stamp by Stampendous
Letter stamp by Limited Edition
Ink pads: black, brown, ochre, rust
Gold embossing powder and embossing pad
Black eyelets
Gold hot glue
Seal

Directions: Emboss plume image on the metallic black-gold paper with clear embossing ink and gold embossing powder. Attach to a 5" x 6³/₈" white folded card. On tan cardstock, stamp the large collage stamp in black. Using the direct-to-paper technique, color with the ochre, rust, and brown ink pads. Mount on black cardstock and set eyelets at each corner. Mount to the card with foam tape. Stamp and emboss the letter image with gold embossing powder on black cardstock. Trim and adhere to the card. Melt two puddles of gold hot glue and stamp with a seal.

CLAY CARDS
By Vanessa Cole

Textured cardstock
Handmade paper (Eco Africa by Provo Craft)
Metallic and printed papers
Black polymer clay
Pearl-Ex powders
Raffia
Ethnic stamps
Pasta machine
Beads and charms
Wire
Melting Pot by Ranger
Glue Dots

Directions: Cut and layer cardstock as desired; set aside. Set melting pot at 350 degrees and keep covered. Take desired amount of clay and condition it through a pasta machine until well blended and shaped to accommodate the size of the stamp which will be impressed in it. Press stamp into clay firmly so that all of the lines of the image are visible. Dip finger into Pearl-Ex powder and rub onto clay image, including the sides. You may use more than one color. Set in melting pot and bake covered for 10–15 minutes. Once cooled, adhere to cardstock using glue dots. Add embellishments (beads, raffia, charms) as desired.

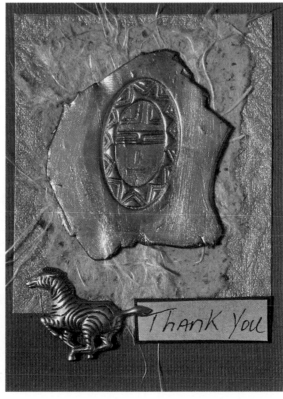

Metal

Beautiful metals of all kinds have been selected by the artists featured here. Wrapped wire, metal foil, accents and coins shimmer and sparkle, extending an invitation to touch.

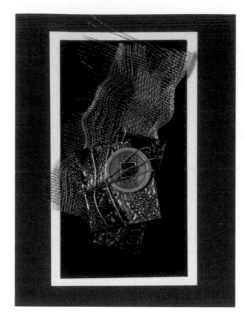

ASIAN COIN CARD
By Barbara Osada

Cardstock: cream, black, red
Piece textured bronze paper
Piece black mat board
Asian coin
Garnet glass bead
Gold mesh ribbon
24-gauge gold wire
Gold & dark green ultra thick embossing powders
Clear embossing ink
Blue microbeads
Gold metallic marker
Tacky glue

Directions: With a gold metallic marker, edge the inside of $4^{1}/_{4}$" x $5^{1}/_{2}$" red card. Layer the black and cream cardstock as shown. Cut a piece of gold mesh ribbon and fray one side. Pull and twist for an irregular shape. Attach with double-sided tape. Layer a $^{7}/_{8}$" x $2^{1}/_{4}$" piece of textured bronze paper over the ribbon. On a $1^{1}/_{4}$" x $1^{1}/_{2}$" piece of black mat board, puddle some clear embossing ink and add the ultra thick embossing powders in gold and dark green. Heat slowly to get a rough texture. Sprinkle some blue microbeads in one corner. Attach coin with hot glue and add garnet bead to center. Randomly wrap with gold wire. Adhere to card with glue.

METAL KIMONO CARD
By Susan Gin

Cardstock: brown, purple, gold
Kimono stamp by Hot Potatoes
Lantern stamp
Bamboo punch by All Night Media
Metal copper sheet, 36-gauge
Purple fiber
Black permanent ink pad
Black pigment ink pad
Black embossing powder
Embossing stylus
Wooden shaping tool
Paper pad or magazine
Double-sided mounting tape

Directions: Stamp kimono stamp using black permanent ink pad on copper sheet and allow to dry; do not use heat tool. With paper pad as a cushion, use stylus to emboss the entire image. Turn over and use wooden shaping tool to "puff out" the image from the back. Cut out image. Heat over burner flame, using a heat-resistant clip. Do not overheat or copper will turn an ashen color. Real copper changes color with high heat; orange, red, and purple hues may appear. Stamp and emboss lanterns on gold paper, using black pigment ink pad and black embossing powder. Cut out lanterns. Punch gold paper on right edge with bamboo punch three times and layer over purple mat. Attach fibers and then adhere lanterns on brown card. Adhere metal kimono to front of card with double-sided mounting tape.

METAL LEAVES
By Susan Gin

Cardstock: caramel, red, metallic bronze
Leaf stamps by Magenta
Metal copper sheet, 36-gauge
Burgundy ribbon
Thank you stamp by Penny Black
Black permanent ink pad
Embossing stylus
Wooden shaping tool
Paper pad or magazine
Metallic copper & black cord
Double-sided mounting tape

Directions: Caramel card has 1$^1/_2$" wide red mat on left side and square metallic bronze mat in the middle. Adhere burgundy ribbon to the card from back to front. Stamp three leaves on the copper sheet using black ink pad. Allow to dry; do not use heat tool. With paper pad as a cushion, use stylus to emboss entire images. Turn over and use wooden shaping tool to "puff out" the images from the back. Cut out leaves. Heat over burner flame, using a heat-resistant clip; do not overheat. Real copper changes color when heated. Let cool. Adhere leaves on card with double-sided mounting tape. Embellish with metallic cord and bow. Stamp "thank you" using black ink pad.

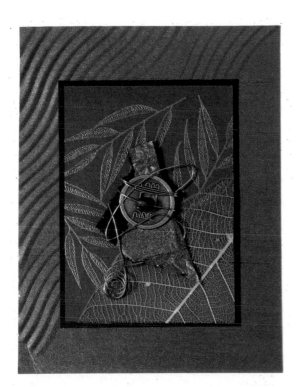

ASIAN COIN AND LEAVES
By Barbara Osada

Cardstock: off-white, navy, black, metallic
     blue
Metallic bronze handmade paper
Scrap of black mat board
Aslan coin
Dark green glass bead
24-gauge gold craft wire
Skeleton leaf
Leaf stamp
Gold embossing powder and clear ink pad
Paper crimper, wave pattern
Tacky glue

Directions: Feed a piece of blue metallic paper at an angle through a paper crimper. Crimp only half way. Glue onto the 4$^1/_4$" x 5$^1/_2$" off-white card. On the navy cardstock, emboss the leaf image with clear embossing ink and gold embossing powder. Adhere the skeleton leaf to the lower corner and trim to card edge. Attach the metallic bronze paper to the scrap of black mat board. Wrap this randomly with the gold wire. Thread the bead and position it to sit in the middle of the coin. Continue to wrap the wire and tape the ends to the back. Glue the coin piece to the card.

SOUTHWESTERN HAPPY BIRTHDAY
By Susan Gin

Cardstock: caramel, rust confetti, black, wheat
Southwest pots stamp by Magenta
Birthday stamp by Hero Arts
Square shadow stamp by Hero Arts
Soft wheat & soft rose ink pads by Memories
Permanent black ink pad
Natural-colored mulberry
Fibers in assorted colors
Paper pad or magazine
Embossing stylus
Wooden shaping tool
Metal copper sheet, 36-gauge
Double-sided foam tape

Directions: Tear a 2" wide piece of mulberry paper and stamp the square shadow stamp using the soft rose ink pad. Stamp again with soft wheat. Stamp the birthday words over the shadow areas using the permanent black ink pad and adhere it to the wheat mat. Layer black and rust mats on the caramel card as shown. Using the permanent ink pad, stamp the southwest pots on the copper sheet and allow to dry; do not use heat tool. With a paper pad as a cushion, use stylus to emboss images of pots. Turn over and use wooden shaping tool to "puff out" the image from the back. Cut out the pots. Heat over burner flame using a heat-resistant clip. Real copper changes color with heat. Overheating results in an ashen color. Allow to cool and adhere to card with double-sided foam tape. Embellish with several colors of fibers.

HEARTFELT THANKS
By Susan Gin

Cardstock: brown, metallic gold
Heart stamp by Magenta
Word stamp
Southwest corner punch
Red fiber
Black permanent ink pad
1/8" hole punch
Embossing stylus
Wooden shaping tool
Paper pad or magazine
Metal copper sheet, 36-gauge
Double-sided foam tape

Directions: Punch corners of the 4" x 5 1/4" gold mat and attach red yarn around all corners. Layer on brown card. Stamp words at top of card, using black ink pad. Stamp heart on copper sheet using black ink pad. Allow to dry; do not use heat tool. With a paper pad as a cushion, use stylus to emboss entire image. Turn over and use wooden shaping tool to "puff out" the image from the back. Cut out the heart. Punch a 1/8" hole at the top of the heart. Heat over burner flame, using a heat-resistant clip. Do not overheat. Real copper changes color with heat. Allow to cool. Embellish with a red bow at the top of the heart. Adhere to the front of the card with double-sided foam tape.

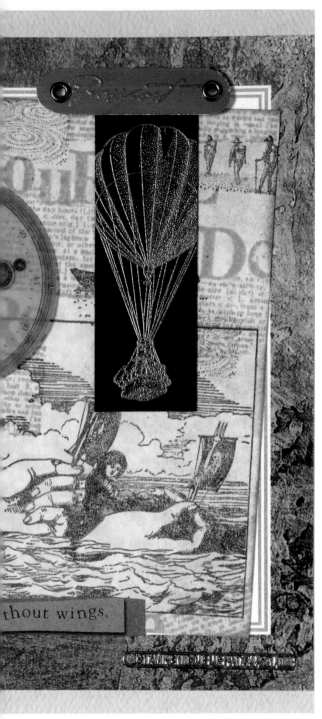

LAYERED PASSPORT
By Barbara Osada

Cardstock: cream, black, gray
Patterned paper
Hand stamp by Above the Mark
Hikers and water by Stampscapes
Hot air balloon by ImaginAir
Text by Limited Edition
Vellum & paper embellishments
Ink pads: black, taupe
Silver embossing powder and embossing pad
Brass eyelets and eyelet tools
Foam tape

Directions: Using a black ink pad, stamp the hand image on cream cardstock. Add the text with taupe ink. Emboss the hot air balloon with clear embossing ink and silver embossing powder on a piece of black cardstock. Layer as shown and add the embellishments. Set the brass eyelets on the passport tag and adhere with foam tape.

THINKING OF YOU
By Susan Gin

Metal copper sheet, 36-gauge
Black permanent ink pad
Round floral stamp by JudiKins
Word stamp
Bronze dragonfly charms
Purple fiber
Circle cutting template by Coluzzle
Embossing stylus
Wooden shaping tool
Paper pad or magazine

Directions: Stamp floral stamp on copper sheet using black ink pad and allow to dry; do not use heat tool. With paper pad as a cushion, use stylus to emboss entire image, then turn over and use the wooden shaping tool to "puff out" the image from the back. Cut out the image. Cut a circle on the front of the caramel card using a Coluzzle circle template. Center and adhere the cut-out image on the purple mat inside caramel card, using double-sided mounting tape. Cut and attach purple strips of matching cardstock to the bottom and right edge of the card as shown. Stamp word stamp using black ink pad and embellish with bronze-colored charms and purple yarn.

Hand-tinting

Coloring enhances images and highlights the artist own special touch. Chalks, inks, paints, and colored pencils each add a delightful accent when applied lovingly by hand.

DRAGONFLY COLLAGE

By Linda Lavasani

Cardstock: purple, orchid, turquoise
180 lb. watercolor paper
Oriental collage stamp by Whispers
Black solvent-based ink
Twinkling H2O's: Passion, Periwinkle,
   Heavenly White, Lime Green, Fern, Gold
Paint brush : $1/2$" flat, soft bristle
Fibers

Directions: Stamp image on watercolor paper using black ink then heat set. Paint the dragonfly wings with Heavenly White and Lime Green. Starting in the left corner and painting to the right, blend Passion, Periwinkle and Fern. Paint the ferns with the color Fern and the medallion with Gold. Paint border with Periwinkle. When dry, closely trim the image, leaving a thin border of white. Layer on the turquoise cardstock, then the orchid and finally the 7" x 5" purple card base. Embellish with fibers.

Second version

Cardstock: black, red, deep teal
180 lb. watercolor paper
Asian calligraphy image
Black solvent-based ink
Twinkling H2O's: Orange Peel, Sunburst,
   Fern, Heavenly White, Garnet
Paint brush: $1/2$" flat, soft bristle
Fibers

Directions: Stamp image on watercolor paper using black ink then heat set. Paint the dragonfly wings with Heavenly White and Fern. Starting in the upper left corner and painting to the right, blend Orange Peel, Sunburst and Fern. Paint the ferns with the color Fern, the medallion with Garnet. Outline with Garnet. When dry, trim the image. Randomly stamp the calligraphy image on the teal cardstock using black ink. Layer the dragonfly image on the teal cardstock, then the red and finally the 7" x 5" black base card. Embellish with fibers.

DRAGONFLY CARD
By Wilda Dupré

Cardstock: white, black
Light blue patterned paper
Dragonfly background stamp by Peddler's
   Pack
Radiant Pearls: London Blue, Snowqueen,
   Cherry Blossom, Dandelion Green
Iridescent glitter glue
Black embossing ink pad
Clear embossing powder

Directions: Emboss dragonfly using black
ink and clear embossing pad on white cardstock. Paint with Radiant Pearls. Apply iridescent glitter glue to waterlilies. Allow
stamped piece to dry. Trim to stamp size.
Adhere to 5^1/$_2$" x 4^1/$_4$" black cardstock and
5" x 7" patterned paper. Adhere to 5^1/$_2$" x
7^1/$_2$" white base card.

SIX WOMEN
By Barbara Osada

Cardstock: sage, lavender, blue, pur-
   ple, white
Women and Swirl Stamp
Line background by Hampton Art
   Stamps
Black dye-based ink pad
Pastel colored pigment ink pads
Markers
Silver embossing powder
Paper crimper
Green craft wire

Directions: On 2^7/$_8$" x 4" blue cardstock,
emboss the swirl image using clear embossing ink and silver embossing powder. Stamp
the background texture with mauve ink on
the 5^1/$_4$" x 4" lavender cardstock piece.
Layer on a 5^1/$_2$" x 4^1/$_4$" sage card. Using a
black ink pad, stamp the women on white
cardstock and cut out. Color with the pastel
ink pads, using the direct-to-paper technique.
Highlight with markers. Add a 2^3/$_8$" x 2" purple background. Crimp the craft wire and coil
the ends. Secure with tape to the card.

POSTAL COLLECTION
By Barbara Osada

Cardstock: khaki, tan, purple, black
Blue textured paper
Scraps of patterned paper
Postal stamps by Hero Arts
Geometric stamp by Paula Best
Black dye-based ink pad
Assorted pigment ink pads
Brass eyelets and setting tools
Decorative scissors
Paper embellishment
Foam tape

Directions: Layer purple, tan, and textured
paper on a 5^1/$_2$" x 4^1/$_4$" khaki folded card.
Add the brass eyelets to the corners of the
4^1/$_2$" x 2^1/$_2$" black cardstock. Stamp an
assortment of postal images from scraps of
cardstock with black ink. Color them with
pigment ink pads using the direct-to-paper
technique. Trim with decorative scissors and
position on the card. Fill in any open spaces
with decorated paper scraps. Add the paper
"journey" embellishment with foam tape for
dimension.

BUTTERFLY CARD
By Wilda Dupré

Cardstock, white, black
Light blue patterned paper
Black Ink pad by Memories
Butterfly background stamp by Peddler's
   Pack
Radiant Pearls: London Blue, Snowqueen,
   Azurite, Summer Sun, Wacky Walnut
Black & iridescent glitter glues
Blue Liquid Pearls

Directions: Stamp butterfly with Memories
black ink pad on white cardstock. Paint
images with Radiant Pearls. Apply black glitter glue to the body of butterfly and apply
iridescent glitter glue to wings. Place dots of
blue Liquid Pearls on edges of wings.
Adhere to 5^1/$_2$" x 4^1/$_4$" black cardstock
and 5" x 7" patterned paper. Adhere to
5^1/$_2$" x 7^1/$_2$" white base card.

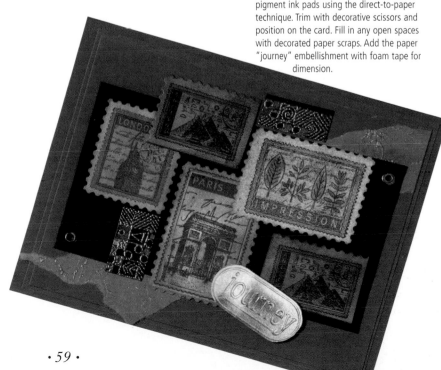

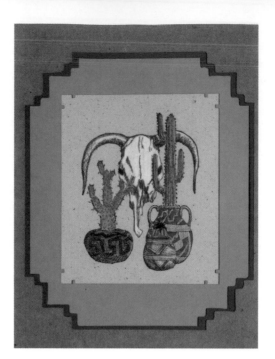

SOUTHWEST
By Terrece Siddoway

Cardstock: mustard, dark grey, turquoise, tan
Deco corner scissors by Fiskars
Southwest corner punch by Marvy
Colored pencils
Black dye-based ink pad
Double-sided tape or glue stick
Southwest stamp by Impression Obsession

Directions: Cut mustard cardstock to $8^1/2$" x $5^1/2$" and fold in half. Stamp image on tan cardstock cut to $2^5/8$" x $3^1/8$". Color with colored pencils. Punch each corner with the southwest corner punch Cut dark grey cardstock to $3^3/4$" x $4^1/2$";, trim each corner with corner scissors. Cut turquoise cardstock to $3^3/4$" x $4^3/8$";, trim each corner with Fiskars corner scissors. Layer with tape or glue stick as shown.

CONTENTED DOGS
By Terrece Siddoway

Cardstock: cream, red, green, mustard
Colored pencils
Black dye-based ink pad
Brown dye-based ink pad
Dogs by Magenta stamp
Background stamp by Rubber Stamp Ave.

Directions: Cut mustard cardstock $10^1/2$" x $5^1/4$" and fold in half to make a $5^1/4$" square card. Stamp background on front of card in brown ink. Stamp dogs on cream cardstock in black ink. Color with colored pencils. Trim image leaving a border around the stamped image. Cut three cream mats: $3^5/8$" square, $2^3/8$" square, $2^1/8$" square. Cut mat from red $3^1/2$" square. Cut mat from green $2^1/4$" square. Attach in order shown.

CRYSTAL BEADED PUMPKIN
By Diana Diaz

Cardstock: moss green, rust, dark green, natural
Stylus
Pumpkin stamp by Personal Stamp Exchange
Tombow pens: shades of green, orange, yellow, gold
Xyron machine with adhesive cartridge
Clear microbeads
Black Brilliance ink pad

Directions: With stylus, emboss a $4^1/2$" frame on a $5^1/2$" square moss green card. Adhere $4^1/8$" rust square and $3^7/8$" green square on card as shown. Stamp pumpkin on $3^5/8$" square natural paper with black Brilliance ink pad. Rub Tombow pens on a palette. Using a brush and a very small amount of water, paint image with Tombow inks. Place image through a Xyron machine to cover the front of the image with adhesive. Remove protective cover and sprinkle with clear microbeads. Adhere image to dark green layer.

GEISHA AND CARP
By Kathy Yee

Cardstock: gold, black, ivory
Asian character background paper
Geisha stamps
Black dye-based ink pad
Radiant Pearls
Double-sided mounting tape

Directions: From gold cardstock make 5 1/2" square base card. Stamp geisha on ivory cardstock with black dye-based ink. Heat set with heat tool. Cut out entire image close to the border. Adhere background paper to gold square card and set aside. Adhere black cardstock to gold cardstock as shown and then adhere the stamped image. Mount piece to the background paper and gold card using double-sided mounting tape. Color the image with Radiant Pearls. Techniques: Point the tip of the brush to the outside edge of the image. Paint around the image by wiggling the brush rather than stroking it. Wet the paintbrush with water then blot off the excess moisture. Draw the Radiant Pearls from the edges to the middle of the image with the dry brush giving it a watercolor effect. Blot excess paint.

ALOHA SHIRT WITH SANDALS
By Barbara Osada

Cardstock: white, off white
Blue window card
Black dye-based ink pad
Light blue ink pad
Aloha shirt stamp by Stamp Yourself Silly
Sandal Stamp by Hanko Designs
Assorted Hawaiian stamps
Colored pencils
Yellow raffia
1/8" hole punch

Directions: Cut a small rectangle of off-white cardstock to fit behind the opening of the blue window card. Randomly stamp various Hawaiian images using a light blue ink pad. Glue in place to the inside of the card. Stamp the Aloha shirt image with black ink on a piece of white cardstock. Color with colored pencils and cut out. Attach to front of the window card. On a piece of light gray cardstock, stamp the sandal image with black ink. Punch a hole at each end and add yellow raffia, tied in a slip knot. Mount below the Aloha shirt.

The Artists

SANDI ALLAN
Originally from South Africa, Sandi is an interior designer and scrapbook artist. She has been scrapbooking for four years. Her hobbies include gardening, sewing, and music. Sandi's two boys and travel inspire her designs.

VANESSA COLE
Vanessa is a former elementary school teacher who is part of the Stamper's Warehouse staff. She has been a rubber stamper for 14 years and a scrapbooker for six years. Vanessa is an avid scrapbooker and book artist who also enjoys fast cars and music. She is passionate about her art and has an ability to translate her emotions into her scrapbook pages.

SUE ASTROTH
Sue, a native Californian, has been stamping and quilting for 20 years. A few years after her move to the Bay Area from Southern California, she joined the Stamper's Warehouse team. Her first book, *Fast and Easy Scrapbook Quilts*, was released in February 2004.

DEBBY DeBENEDETTI
Since 1998, Debby has enjoyed the creative challenges scrapbooking offers. She enjoys teaching techniques that stretch her abilities as well as those of her students. She is married and has two sons, Anthony and Cade.

TRACI BAUTISTA
A California mixed media artist, art educator and graphic designer, Traci believes that there is an "artist" in everyone. She is an artist-in-residence at the Palo Alto Art Center and also teaches workshops at paper art stores in California. Traci sells her unique hand-painted papers and one-of-a-kind aRt! kits for art journaling and stamping.

DIANA DIAZ
After 13 years of teaching rubber stamp classes, Diana is still going strong. She has been associated with Stamper's Warehouse from its beginning. Because of Diana's enthusiasm, many of her tennis students have found their way to rubber stamping. Diana's cards showcase the amazing possibilities of stamping techniques.

PATTY CARLSON
Patty has been a rubber stamper and paper crafter for ten years. She loves the way stamping has evolved as an art form and especially enjoys making pieces with Asian themes. Despite her demanding, full-time job, Patty indulges in her rubber stamp "addiction" almost every day. Her beautiful creations attest to her love and dedication.

SUSAN GIN
Susan has been stamping for 14 years. She worked and taught at Stamper's Warehouse for seven years. Susan has always been eager to try the newest techniques in the stamping world. Since she no longer lives near Stamper's Warehouse, Susan stamps with her friends and neighbors.

KRISTA HALLIGAN

In 2001 Krista joined the creative team at Stamper's Warehouse where her expertise has flourished. She has been stamping and scrapbooking for 9 years. Drawn to art and the creative process, she especially enjoys working on projects which reveal their own direction and themes during their creation.

LINDA LAVASANI

Linda's background has been in the banking and lending industry. She didn't discover her hidden artistic talents until she began rubber stamping in 1995. That is still her first love. She also enjoys refinishing furniture, designing polymer clay and beaded jewelry, and creating collage pieces.

PHYLLIS NELSON

Phyllis, the creative force behind Stamper's Warehouse, enjoys sharing her love of stamping with her talented staff and customers. Her extensive experience with stamping and card-making is witnessed in her elegant style and versatile techniques.

BARBARA OSADA

Barb was an Art Major at San Jose State. She lost touch with art after working in accounting and bookkeeping while raising her children. Barb discovered the Stamper's Warehouse nine years ago. Barb is now a full-time stamper who looks at everything in terms of how it could be used in her cards. Barb loves collage and ethnic themes. She is also an avid knitter.

TERRECE SIDDOWAY

Born in Idaho, Terrece graduated from Brigham Young University. She began stamping ten years ago. In addition to her job as store manager at Stamper's Warehouse, she teaches many popular classes in stamping and scrapbooking. Terrece's love of all things western is reflected in her projects. Her dog, Angel, assists in all of her creations.

BECKIE TORGERSON

Beckie is a documentation supervisor at a local manufacturer. Throughout her life, she has been involved in many crafts. In the last ten years Beckie has concentrated on stamping. Beckie works on a technique until she has perfected it and gives it her own personal touch.

KATHY YEE

Kathy is a program manager for a semiconductor equipment company who enjoys stamping as a hobby. She was introduced to stamping by her old college roommate seven years ago and hasn't stopped since. Kathy enjoys stamping because it combines structure and creativity. She's been teaching for three years and her specialty is Asian designs.

WITH ADDITIONAL PROJECTS BY:

Connie Baldonado

Wilda Dupré

Jenn Gaub

Stacie Enriquez

Ailene Lew

Sandi Marr

Gail Martin

Janis Ramsden

Susan Thompson

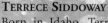

Resources

Many of the products used in this book are available at your local craft and/or scrapbook retailer. Products may also be purchased through Stamper's Warehouse. For assistance in locating a retailer in your area, consult the companies below.

Note: Some of the stamped images and papers shown may no longer be available from the manufacturers. Stamps and papers from other companies may be used to achieve the same effects.

STAMPER'S WAREHOUSE
101-G Town & Country Dr.
Danville, CA 94526
925-262-9595
Fax 925-362-0999
www.stamperswarehouse.com
Class schedule available online

STAMP COMPANIES
A Stamp in the Hand
All Night Media
Above the Mark
Art Impressions
Curtis Uyeda
Dreamweaver
Dolphin Song
Fred Mullett
Hampton Art Stamp
Hanko Designs
Heartfelt Impressions
Hero Arts
Holly Berry House
Hot Potatoes
Inkadinkado
ImaginAir Designs
Impression Obsession
Invoke Arts
JudiKins
Leavenworth Jackson
Magenta
Make an Impression
Paper Inspirations
Paper Parachute
Paula Best
Peddler's Pack
Penny Black
Personal Stamp Exchange
Rubber Stampede
Rubber Stamps of America
Rubber Stamp Ave.
Stamp Out Cute
Stampland
Stamp Francisco
Stampington
Stamp Yourself Silly
Stamper's Anonymous
Stampendous
Stampscapes
Stamp Zia
Whispers by Sugarloaf

ANGELWINGS – *Radiant Pearls*
3322 W. Sussex Way
Fresno, CA 93722
866-229-1544
www.radiantpearls.com

CLEARSNAP, INC. – *ColorBox ink pads, embossing pads*
P.O. Box 98
Anacortes, WA 98221
800-448-4862
www.clearsnap.com

ECSTASY CRAFTS
P.O. Box 525
Watertown, NY 13601
888-288-7131
www.ecstasycrafts.com

EMAGINATION CRAFTS
504 Wrightwood Blvd.
Elmhurst, IL 60126
866-238-9770

FISKARS MFG. CORP. – *paper crimper, decorative scissors, cutting tools*
7811 Stewart Ave.
Wausau, WI 54401-9071
715-842-2091
www.fiskars.com

GOLDEN ARTISTS COLORS, INC. – *glazes, acrylic paints, artist mediums*
188 Bell Road
New Berlin, NY 13411
607-847-6154
www.goldenpaints.com

JACQUARD – *Lumiere, Neopaque, textile paint, Pearl-Ex*
Rupert Gibbon & Spider
P.O. Box 425
Healdsburg, CA 95448
707-433-9577
www.jacquardproducts.com

KRYLON – *metallic leafing pens, spray adhesive, spray fixatives*
101 Prospect Ave. NW
Cleveland, OH 44115
216-515-7693
www.krylon.com

LEISURE ARTS, INC. – *paper, books*
5701 Ranch Drive
Little Rock, AR 72223
800-643-8030
www.leisurearts.com

MAKING MEMORIES
P.O. Box 1188
Centerville UT 84014
800-286-5263
www.makingmemories.com

MARVY UCHIDA – *Liquid Appliqué, cutt mats, punches, pens, heat tools*
3535 Del Amo Blvd.
Torrance, CA 90503
800-541-5877
www.uchida.com

POLYFORM PRODUCTS CO. – *Premo polymer clay, molds, Sculpey glaze*
1901 Estes Ave.
Elk Grove Village, IL 60007
847-427-0020
www.sculpey.com

PROVO CRAFT
151 East 3450 North
Spanish Fork, UT 84660
800-937-7686
www.provocraft.com

RANGER INDUSTRIES, INC. – *Adironda ink pads, Melting Pot, UTEE, craft sheets Perfect Pearls, Nick Bantock ink pads*
15 Park Rd.
Tinton Falls, NJ 07724
908-389-3535

7GYPSIES
877-7GYPSY7
www.sevengypsies.com

TSUKINEKO
17640 NE 65th St.
Redmond, WA 98052
800-769-6633
www.tsukineko.com

USArtQUEST
7800 Ann Arbor Rd.
Grass Lake, MI 49240
800-200-7848

XYRON – *machines and refills for applying adhesive*
15820 N. 84th St.
Scottsdale, AZ 85260
800-793-3523
www.xyron.com